Artful Ways with Polymer Clay

DOTTY McMILLAN

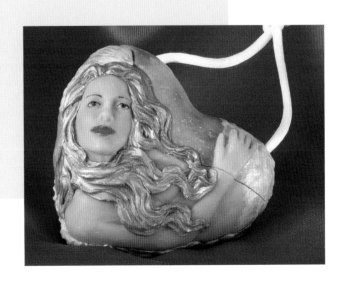

Sterling Publishing Co., Inc.
New York

This book is dedicated to my family and friends, whose constant encouragement and suggestions have enabled me to complete it. And especially to Al, for always being there.

ACKNOWLEDGMENTS

I am most grateful to the members of the Orange County Polymer Clay Guild, the San Diego Polymer Clay Guild, and the members of the National Polymer Clay Guild for their wonderful encouragement and friendship. My deepest gratitude also goes to my editor, Isabel Stein, for all her help and patience.

A very special thank-you to Polyform Products for donating a great deal of the Premo! clay used for the projects in the book, as well as to Donna Kato and Van Aken International for donating both Kato Polyclay and liquid clay for the book. And to the Lazertran Company, who supplied most of the transfer paper used for this book.

All photos by Michael Hnatov except for gallery photos and those by the author: pages 15, 16 and 17; page 25, left; page 26, right; page 27; page 29; page 30, left.

Library of Congress Cataloging-in-Publication Data
McMillan, Dotty.
 Artful ways with polymer clay / Dotty McMillan.
  p. cm.
 Includes index.
 ISBN 1-4027-0282-5
 1. Polymer clay craft. I. Title.

 TT297.M395 2004
 731.4'2—dc22

                    2004018558

          10 9 8 7 6 5 4 3 2

Published by Sterling Publishing Co., Inc.
387 Park Avenue South, New York, NY 10016
©2006 by Dotty McMillan
Distributed in Canada by Sterling Publishing
℅ Canadian Manda Group, 165 Dufferin Street
Toronto, Ontario, Canada M6K 3H6
Distributed in the United Kingdom by GMC Distribution Services,
Castle Place, 166 High Street, Lewes, East Sussex, England BN7 1XU
Distributed in Australia by Capricorn Link (Australia) Pty. Ltd.
P.O. Box 704, Windsor, NSW 2756, Australia

Sterling ISBN 1-4027-0282-5

For information about custom editions, special sales, premium and
corporate purchases, please contact Sterling Special Sales
Department at 800-805-5489 or specialsales@sterlingpub.com.

Contents

Tools,
Supplies &
Basic
Information

What could be more creative than playing with brightly colored pieces of soft clay and turning them into stunning works of art? Imagine wearing jewelry that you have made to match every outfit you own, adorning a variety of household items with delightful images, and creating fan pulls and doorknobs to go with your bedroom or bathroom. Maybe you would enjoy fashioning tiny kaleidoscopes to wear, brightly colored masks for fun or decoration, funky picture frames, sleek teapots and containers, unique clocks, or your own treasure trove of bright, colorful beads. All of this is possible and easy with the new-age medium called polymer clay. This book will take you from the very basics all the way to some of the latest techniques.

HOW IT BEGAN

Polymer clay, although still in its infancy, is now recognized as an art medium that has had the power to capture the imagination of thousands of artists almost instantly. Why? Because polymer clay has far more potential for diversity than any other art medium. Once you start working with it, you'll quickly discover its unique and amazing qualities. Polymer clay is new on the art scene, compared to mediums such as earthen clays, oil paints, wood, and precious metals. It was born in the era when plastics were being developed. An early plastic called Bakelite, developed by Belgian chemist Dr. Leo H. Baekeland in 1907, started the craze for all things plastic. Polymer clay is one of the "after Bakelite" plastics, to which it owes its existence.

In the latter part of the 1930s, a woman in Germany by the name of "Fifi" Rehbinder was looking for the necessary materials to make doll heads. During her experiments, she discovered a clay-like byproduct and named it Fifi Mosaik after her nickname. She began her own business, marketing the clay, and did so until 1964, when she went to the German company Eberhard Faber with it. At that time, the product we now know as FIMO™ polymer clay was born. Later, several other companies began to manufacture their own brands of polymer clay. Today, polymer clay is available in a variety of brands, each with its own unique characteristics, and in a rainbow of colors.

1. Sunday's Ride by Kathy Davis.

You'll find it surprisingly easy to work with. Mold and shape it by hand, and use all sorts of everyday items to form and texture it. Silk-screen it with colorful patterns, and highlight it with image transfers. Discover how to make a variety of faux materials such as jade, turquoise, ivory, wood, and polished or aged metal. Bundle rods of color together to form colorful millefiori pattern canes. Appliqué, stamp, carve, saw, sand, and buff it. Mix in a variety of inclusions, such as spices from the kitchen, for unique effects. Use the clay for painting pictures or forming mosaics; shape it into lamps, vessels, boxes, and purses; or turn it into buttons, beads, and beautiful baubles. What more could an artist or crafter possibly want?

WHAT IS POLYMER CLAY?

Polymer clay is a smooth, soft claylike plastic that is easily coaxed into just about any shape. It can then be baked in a home oven to become a stable and durable object that retains its shape.

Unlike earthen clay, polymer clay was developed in a chemist's laboratory. It is a form of the thermosetting plastic known as polyvinyl chloride (PVC), which is used to make such things as plumbing pipes. The PVC is mixed with colored pigments and plasticizers to make it workable. The term thermosetting means that it is set into a solid form by heat, after which it can't be reformed. When the clay is baked at a temperature range from 212°F to 275°F (100°C to 135°C), it undergoes chemical changes. The particles fuse into a solid shape, and the shape is retained.

Polymer clay comes in various kinds, including: opaque colors, translucent colors, colorless translucent, liquid translucent, liquid opaque white, a form that remains flexible and stretchy after baking, stone and granite types, and a form that absorbs light and glows in the dark.

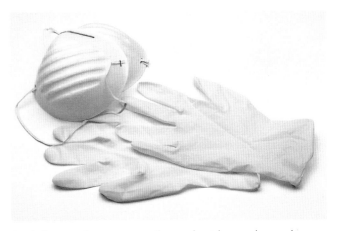

3. A face mask is important for work with powders such as mica and powdered metals. Rubber gloves are used by some people to protect their hands, if they are allergic to the chemicals in polymer clay.

2. Liquid clay and a variety of colors of polymer clay.

SAFETY ISSUES

Every so often you may hear someone make claims that polymer clay is toxic and is not safe to use. This is not true according to the ACMI (Art & Creative Materials Institute, Inc.), an international organization that is responsible for a program that checks to see that art materials are nontoxic and meet certain standards of quality and performance. The ACMI reviews the formulas of all products included within the certification program. You can check the status of various polymer clays at *www.acminet.org*.

According to these experts, polymer clay has been ruled safe to use as long as a few simple safety rules are followed.

❖ The first rule with polymer clay is not to eat it or let your children eat it. Your tools and equipment should be reserved for working with polymer clay and should never be used for food. Items made of polymer clay should not be used for food, either.

❖ Polymer clay should not be used by children under 5, who might eat it. Play dough made from flour, salt, and food coloring can be used for young children instead.

❖ It's important to use an oven thermometer for an accurate reading of how hot your oven is, to avoid burning. Like most plastics, if it is overheated, polymer clay will turn dark or burn and give off noxious fumes, which should not be inhaled. If something burns, air out the room and leave the room until the fumes have gone.

❖ The clay can be baked in your home oven if you are doing only a small amount of work. If you do a considerable amount, it would be wise to invest in a toaster oven or a convection oven that is used only for polymer clay.

❖ If possible, set the oven up outside the house: in a garage, patio, etc. The next best solution is to place it in a room that has an open window, one that will not be occupied when your work is baking. It's best not to breathe in the fumes that come off while polymer clay is baking. Also, if your polymer clay burns, the fumes will be away from your main living/eating area, and cleanup will be easier. It's a good idea to have a fire extinguisher nearby, just in case you need it.

❖ Caution: Never put polymer clay in the microwave or under a direct flame such as a broiler.

❖ When sanding the clay, use wet/dry sandpaper with water so that the polymer dust isn't inhaled or spread around to possibly contaminate food.

❖ Always wear a mask when working with powdered metals or mica.

❖ When buffing your items on a buffing wheel, wear a face mask, as painters do, to avoid inhaling the residue, and wear safety glasses.

❖ After using polymer clay, wash your hands carefully. You can use baby wipes, baby oil, or isopropyl alcohol, followed by soap and water.

❖ If your skin appears to be sensitive to the unbaked clay, wear thin, tight latex or rubber gloves while working with it.

TOOLS AND SUPPLIES

If you are just beginning to work with polymer clay, you'll find you can achieve a great deal with basic tools. Here are some suggested items to get you started.

1. Work surface: A large tile, heavy piece of glass or Plexiglas™ or another smooth sturdy surface.

2. A sharp blade: Tissue blades or other sharp steel blades are recommended and are now available from a variety of craft supply places. A blade about ¾" (1.6 cm) wide and 4" to 6" (10 to 15 cm) long is ideal. It is a little thicker than an industrial razor blade, and is flexible enough to bend.

3. Roller or brayer: Choose one made of Plexiglas, acrylic, marble, or any roller that has an extremely smooth surface. Avoid wooden rollers as they usually leave marks.

4. Oven: Your regular home oven is fine if you are not going to do a great many pieces. Get a toaster oven or a convection oven and reserve it for clay use if you are going to do a lot of work.

4. Some helpful clay tools. Top row, left to right: hand carving tools, hand drill, craft knife, needle; clay tool, pasta machine. Middle left, Dremel tool, with attachments. In front, left to right: brayer and acrylic roller, cutting blades (tissue blades), small grater, and shaping tools.

5. Polymer clay: See pages 10 to 12 for the different kinds available. Many projects list the kinds you will need for that project.

6. Oven thermometer: For checking to make sure your oven temperature is correct. This is crucial, as the dial temperatures on ovens sometimes are inaccurate.

7. Baking surface: This could be a paper-covered metal or heatproof glass pan or sheet, or a ceramic tile.

8. Needle or needle tool and drill: For making holes in beads and other things.

9. Carving tools such as linoleum cutters: For cutting lines and shapes into clay.

10. Pasta machine: You can manage without it; however, your hands will be glad if you get one. It is used for rolling out smooth, even sheets of clay in various thicknesses and for conditioning the clay and mixing colors. It should be dedicated to polymer clay and not be used for food.

11. Steel ruler: Helps when cutting straight lines or measuring canes. One with millimeters on it would be helpful.

12. Graph paper: For use in measuring, enlarging, and cutting pieces of clay.

13. Buffing wheel or buffing cloth: For bringing up a shine on the surface of the clay.

14. Very fine steel wool (0000): Used for buffing to a matte finish.

15. A variety of objects for texturing, such as carved buttons, Phillips screwdriver, thick-toothed comb, rough tree bark, etc.

16. Specially designed texture screens for use with polymer clay: To either texture the surface or to penetrate deeply into unbaked clay for certain techniques.

17. Fire extinguisher: A handy thing to have around, in the rare event that your clay catches fire.

18. Mold release: For example, talc, cornstarch, Armorall™, or water. Helps to keep raw clay from sticking to molds, rubber stamps, and other molding objects.

19. Wet/dry sandpaper in various grits from 220 to 2000 grit, including 320, 400, and 600: For smoothing the surface of baked clay and rounding off or smoothing rough edges. Sanding wet minimizes the amount of dust in the air, which is healthier.

20. Dust mask: To wear while buffing or working with powders.

21. Safety glasses: To wear while buffing or sanding.

22. Extruder such as clay gun: To press out various shapes of clay and long, stringlike pieces.

23. Parchment paper, tracing paper, or bakery paper: To make lifting and turning pieces of clay easier, for baking in oven, tracing, etc.

24. Aluminum foil: For shaping interiors of various pieces to reduce their weight.

25. Cookie cutters, and small aspic cutters or Kemper tools: For cutting various shapes.

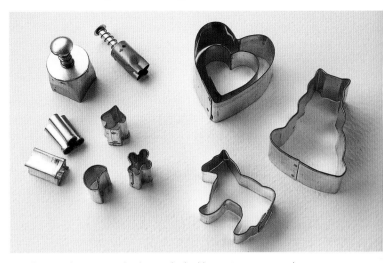

6. Cutters for use with clay include Kemper cutters and cookie cutters.

26. Rubber stamps: For texturing the surface of the clay and for creating images on the surface of the clay. You can make stamps yourself (see Making Rubber Stamps, page 20) or buy them.

27. Molds: For easy shaping of the clay. Available in faces, leaves, flowers, etc. Or make your own (see Making Molds, pages 21 to 24).

28. Clay modeling tools: For sculpting.

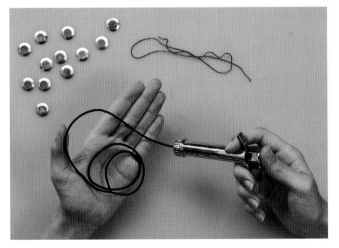

5. Clay gun, used for making thin ropes of clay, in various shapes.

7. Stamps, molds, and colored pencils are all used in working with polymer clay.

29. Metallic foils: Real or imitation gold, silver, or copper foils. To use as adornment on or under the clay surface. The imitation ones are used by most people as they are much less expensive. However, real gold foil tends to keep its color better over long periods of time.

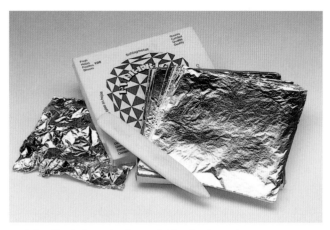

8. Metallic foils and a bone folder for burnishing.

30. Metallic or mica powders and embossing powders. To use on or in unbaked clay to produce a colorful sheen or metallic effect. Available in a wide variety of colors.

31. Acrylic paints: For antiquing baked clay and doing other paint techniques, such as silk-screening. Burnt sienna and burnt umber are popular colors for antiquing.

32. Small paintbrushes: For antiquing, glazing, painting, and applying powders.

33. Colored pencils: For coloring black-and-white transfers, planning colors, etc.

34. Scissors, regular and patterned: For trimming or edging both baked and unbaked clay, cutting out patterns, etc.

35. Leafing pens: Gold, silver, and copper pens for drawing on or highlighting baked clay. Not all brands work on polymer clay. Krylon brand is one that is compatible with the clay.

36. Metallic wax: A rub-on substance to give baked clay the appearance of metal.

37. Mineral oil or diluent (the latter is sold by the clay companies): For conditioning clay that is too hard and crumbly.

38. Clay-compatible glazes or finishes: Sculpey glaze, FIMO mineral-based glaze, Flecto Diamond Varathane Elite, and Future acrylic floor finish are some examples.

39. Polyester stuffing (the kind used for stuffing toys or quilts): For holding rounded objects while they bake, and to avoid flat spots on the bottom of an object.

40. Jewelry findings: Necklace closures, pin backs, and cords or bead wires for jewelry. See individual projects for specifics.

41. Bead supports: Wooden skewers, wire, or knitting needles to hold beads when baking.

With the above-listed items, you can get to know the clay and be able to do a great many exciting projects. Once you've worked with the clay for awhile, you'll discover many more items that you'll find helpful. A few are:

1. Mini food processor: If you are using one of the harder clays, such as FIMO™ Classic, this is an excellent way to start conditioning. Use for clay only, not food.

2. Dremel™ tool: For drilling holes or buffing, using a buffing attachment.

3. Noodle cutter: For cutting long, even strips of clay.

4. Dental tools: For modeling and sculpting.

5. Inclusions such as dried herbs, colored sand, or tiny beads. To color and texture clay.

6. Color wheel: An aid in mixing and combining colors of clay.

7. Garlic press: For making narrow strings of clay, often used for hair on small figures.

8. Mini grater: For making tiny bits of clay.

WHICH CLAY SHOULD YOU CHOOSE?

Polymer clay comes in a variety of brands. Each has a slightly different texture and qualities. All of the brands are excellent. Try each of them and choose the ones you find easiest to work with that result in colors and surfaces that please you. Some of the projects in this book call for specific clays that I feel work best for that particular technique or project; see individual projects for details. Many artists use several brands and types of clay, depending upon the projects. Here are some of the ones available.

❖ Sculpey III™ (by Polyform Products Co., Elk Grove Village, Illinois) comes in a great many colors and is the softest and easiest of the polymer clays to condition. This clay isn't as strong when baked as some of the others. However, despite its weakness, many clay artists have created beautiful works of art with it.

❖ Premo! Sculpey™ was developed especially for the polymer clay artist by Polyform Products Co. and Marie Segal of The Clay Factory of Escondido, California. Premo! is medium soft and easy to condition. It holds cane patterns fairly well and is extremely strong and somewhat flexible after baking. It comes in a wide variety of artist's colors, which change very little or not at all after baking.

❖ FIMO™, manufactured by Eberhard Faber in Germany, is now available in a FIMO Soft version, which is much easier to condition than the original FIMO, and in FIMO Classic, which has the characteristics of the original FIMO. FIMO Classic can sometimes be difficult to condition, but it holds cane patterns extremely well. Baking gives it a very nice matte finish. FIMO is quite strong after baking.

❖ Kato Polyclay™ (Van Aken International, Rancho Cucamonga, California) is the newest addition to the brands of polymer clay that are available. Kato Polyclay is easy to condition and has a smooth texture and a non-sticky consistency. There is very little color change when baked. It slices very cleanly with little distortion, which makes it excellent clay for canemaking. It comes in eight spectral colors, which can be mixed to make just about any other colors you might want. Four neutrals and four metallics, plus translucent also are offered.

9. Sculpture by Pam Rouleau.

❖ Cernit™, manufactured by T & F GmBH in Germany, is the strongest of the clays and develops a lovely porcelainlike surface after it is baked. It is a favorite of many dollmakers. Some of its colors are very intense, but diluting them with white gives wonderful results. Dollmakers often use a mixture of Cernit and Super Sculpey clay, which is beige, for a very workable and attractive finish.

❖ Super Sculpey™ (Polyform Products Co.) is a strong beige-toned clay that comes in large blocks. It can be used for figures that are going to be painted, as a base to which you may apply cane slices or other decorations, or mixed with Cernit or other flesh-colored clay for dollmaking.

❖ Sculpey™ SuperFlex (Polyform Products Co.) is an extremely soft clay to work with, and it remains quite flexible after baking. It is especially good for making molds with undercuts.

❖ Translucent Liquid Sculpey® (Polyform Products Co.), or TLS for short, is a liquid form of polymer clay that can be used as a surface enhancement, as an aid to help adhere baked and unbaked pieces together during the second baking, and as a transfer medium.

It can be colored with oil paint, pigments, mica powders, and embossing powders.

❖ Kato Liquid Medium Polyclay (Von Aken) is a fairly new liquid clay. It is somewhat different from Translucent Liquid Sculpey. It is more transparent and has a smoother, shinier finish after baking. It is a little more difficult to sand, but adding a small amount of liquid dishwashing soap to your sanding water helps greatly. Kato Medium can be used for the same techniques as Translucent Liquid Sculpey.

❖ FIMO now offers a form of liquid clay called Liquid Decorating Gel, which is very transparent when baked.

The type of clay one uses can be a very personal thing, so be sure you are working with one that suits you.

CONDITIONING THE CLAY

In order to have strength and stability, polymer clay should be conditioned before it is used. This is necessary even if the clay you choose is soft and workable when you first open it. Nowadays, conditioning is not difficult and should not take much time. Before the discovery that a mini-food processor and a pasta machine made this job quite easy, most artists conditioned clay completely by hand. You can still do this job by hand if you prefer, or if the expense of a machine is too much for your budget.

Conditioning by hand: Warm the clay before beginning by placing a packet of clay next to your body warmth. Under your arm or in the waistband of your skirt or slacks will do the trick. Or set it on a bun warmer or heating pad. Don't overdo the warming or your clay will begin to bake. Work only small pieces of the clay at a time to condition. Roll the clay out into a long snake, fold it in half, twist it together, roll into a ball, and repeat this process a number of times, until the clay is smooth and workable.

Conditioning by machine: For clay that is not hard and crumbly, run it through the pasta machine on the thickest setting, fold it in half, and run it through again, folded end first. Repeat this process until the clay is smooth and workable. If the clay is hard and crumbly, cut it into small chunks, drop them into a mini food processor, and run the processor for about 25 seconds or until the clay is warm and has turned into tiny balls. If the clay feels very dry, add one or two drops of mineral oil or one of the additives put out by the clay companies for this purpose (Sculpey Diluent by Polyform or Quick-Mix by FIMO). Don't add too much diluent to begin with, as you can easily make your clay way too soft and sticky. Remove the clay from the processor and press it into a patty that is thin enough to go through the thickest setting on the pasta machine. Roll it through the machine and fold the clay; repeat until it is smooth and doesn't crack when folded.

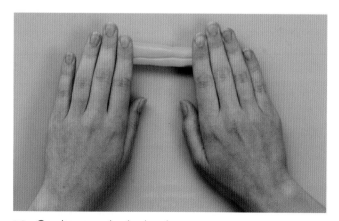

10. Conditioning clay by hand.

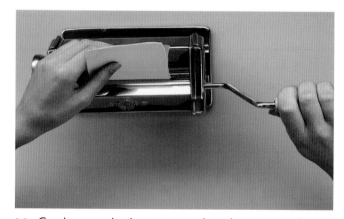

11. Conditioning clay by running it through a pasta machine.

SOME MEASUREMENTS

Many projects suggest using a pasta machine for rolling sheets of clay to a desired thickness. If you don't have a pasta machine, you can roll clay with an acrylic or marble rolling pin or printer's brayer, using a ruler to check the thickness of the sheets. The settings on pasta machines aren't standardized, so if you use one, do some tests to see what thickness you get on each setting of your machine, and make a little setting chart for yourself if the thicknesses are different from those in the chart given here, which is based on my Atlas pasta machine. We will use settings and thicknesses throughout the book, so even if your settings are different, you will know what thickness of clay to roll.

Pasta Machine Settings*

Settings	Inches	mm
#1	⅛	3.2
#2	⁷⁄₆₄	2.8
#3	³⁄₃₂	2.4
#4	⁵⁄₆₄	2
#5	¹⁄₁₆	1.6
#6	¹⁄₃₂	0.8
#7	¹⁄₄₀	0.6

*Based on the author's pasta machine.

BAKING THE CLAY

Manufacturers of polymer clays include guidelines with the clays on what oven temperature to use. The goal is to get the small polymer clay particles hot enough to fuse together, but not so hot that they burn. Thin objects get heated through faster than thick ones. Thick objects may burn on the outside but not be fused on the inside if the temperature is too high. Different clays have different recommended baking times and temperatures, and with some brands, such as FIMO and Sculpey III, translucents have different recommended baking temperatures than opaque colors.

Here are several things to keep in mind:

1. Use an oven thermometer, rather than relying on the oven dial's calibrations, which frequently are inaccurate. Each oven is slightly different from the others. An increase of even 25°F (13°C) can be the difference between baking well and overbaking (turning brown) or underbaking.

2. Preheat the oven to the correct temperature before inserting your pieces, unless a project specifically suggests you use a cool oven. With most convection ovens, however, this isn't always necessary.

3. Bake your clay pieces on a surface that doesn't conduct heat well, such as a ceramic tile, parchment paper, card stock, or an ovenproof dish that is reserved for clay only (not used for food). Don't place the pieces too close to the heating element. A metal pan should have parchment or regular paper on its surface. In some cases, use a "nest" of polyester batting to rest your piece on; this will be indicated in the project's instructions.

4. For each new clay you use, bake a few sample squares at various temperatures and thicknesses, to see what temperature to use at the thickness you are planning. Label and save these squares for future reference.

5. Transparent and flesh tones of FIMO and Sculpey need to be baked at a lower temperature (212°F, 100°C) than the other colors. When you add one-fourth or more FIMO translucent or Sculpey III translucent to a color, you should use the translucent temperature recommended by the manufacturer. However, if you add less than that, it's best to bake at

12. A portable oven thermometer is important for assuring the correct oven temperature.

the temperature recommended for the colored clay. Otherwise the colored clay won't be properly cured.

6. Don't bake polymer clay in a microwave oven or put it under a broiler.

7. In the event of a fire, put out the fire with a fire extinguisher or baking soda, open the windows to get rid of the fumes, and leave the room until the fumes have cleared.

COLOR MIXING

In the world of art, color is probably the most important factor. Many people are afraid of using color for fear they will do it "wrong." However, take a look at the natural world. Nature isn't afraid of being bold or of mixing various colors in one palette. The task of artists is to discover which colors they are comfortable working with, and which colors work well together. Even colors that you might think clash can be modified to go with each other. Take your cues from nature and don't be afraid to jump in and experiment. You'll be surprised at what you discover.

Some brands of polymer clay offer a great variety of premixed colors, while some offer fewer and encourage you to mix your own variations. With any brand, it's possible to extend your color palette by learning how easy it is to mix colors. Below are some suggestions. The color names listed here are mostly Premo! clay names, but similar colors from other brands will work just as well.

Mixing with Pearl Clays

Pearl clays contain mica. Mix plain pearl clay 50/50 with almost any other color, including black. The more pearl, the softer the color and more pearlescent it will be. The less pearl, the brighter the color. Here are a few mixes to try:

50/50 Premo! Gold pearl clay with cadmium red. This makes a luscious golden-red fit for a queen.
50/50 Premo! gold pearl with silver pearl for an unusual effect.
75/25 Gold pearl with purple for a lovely shade of purple.
50/50 Gold pearl with green. Gorgeous!
50/50 Gold pearl with turquoise.
75/25 Gold pearl with ultramarine.
50/50 Silver pearl with plain pearl for luminous platinum.
50/50 Silver with any yellow. Light and bright.
50/50 Copper with cadmium red. Really polished copper!
50/50 Silver with any blue, green, or purple.
50/50 Black and gold for a lush bronze.
50/50 Red pearl and blue pearl for a lustrous grape purple.
A swirled mixture of Bordeaux Red with plain pearl makes strawberries and cream.

You get the idea. Now try every other combination you can think of. Keep a record! You'll be glad you did!

Mixing with Translucent Clay

Beautiful translucent colors can be made by blending a small amount of any of the opaque clays with translucent. The trick here is to start with just a small amount of the opaque color. To 2 oz (56 g) of translucent, add a rice grain amount of the color clay. Mix. Continue adding small amounts until you reach the saturation you want. As a rule, baking will somewhat deepen the color. If you add too much color you will lose the translucent effect.

Mix glow-in-the-dark clay with just about any other color of translucent or opaque clay and see what you can come up with. It will lighten the other color, but in a different way than white does. The less of the second color you use, the more your mix will be able to glow in the dark.

Mixing Opaque Colors

Hundreds of color variations can be made by mixing a variety of opaque colors. The principles of mixing oil or watercolor paints work quite nicely for the clay. It pays to experiment and keep a journal of your experiments; otherwise, you will come up with an absolutely gorgeous color and never be able to repeat it. Page 16 has some starter ideas to try.

13. Bracelet made using techniques developed by Christie Friesen; by Dotty McMillan.

14. Colorful Fish Pendant was made using techniques developed by clay artist Christie Friesen; by Dotty McMillan.

❖ Cadmium red and alizarin crimson 50/50 make a lovely red.

❖ Fluorescent (any color): add to another color in small amounts to brighten. Cool down fluorescent colors by adding ecru, beige, or champagne.

❖ Desaturate any color (make it less intense, or grayer) by mixing in a small amount of its complementary color (the one opposite it on the color wheel). For example, make bright green less intense by mixing in a little orange.

❖ For soft Early American colors, add some Super Sculpey (beige) to any other color.

❖ Add a warm yellow and a touch of brown to white for a quick ivory.

❖ Blend 50/50 ecru or beige into most colors for a soft, dusty, rather southwestern color.

❖ Mix raw sienna and cadmium yellow for a nice tan.

❖ Mix any green with a small amount of white and black to make Celadon green.

❖ Try 50/50 sap or leaf green and ultramarine for a Hunter type of green.

❖ Add a little violet to any medium blue for a periwinkle shade of blue.

❖ A mix of ultramarine blue and alizarin crimson comes close to a Wedgwood blue. Add small amounts of white until you reach the exact shade you want.

❖ Fluorescent pink mixed with purple in various amounts. Yummy purples.

❖ Alizarin crimson and various amounts of white. Delicious berry colors.

❖ Magenta and a warm yellow make for a beautiful coral.

❖ Cadmium red with a small amount of black make for a brick tone.

This list could go on for pages, but this much should get you started on the road to the great fun and satisfaction to be found in mixing your own colors.

ARTFUL WAYS WITH POLYMER CLAY

Experimenting with Color

Some people seem more comfortable working primarily with a specific color palette, while others love to jump from one to another. Do some experimenting to see what you come up with. One of the best ways to start is by making a variety of clay bead color swatches.

Every brand of clay has several reds, blues, and yellows, which are your primary colors. By using various combinations of these, you can create a variety of color blends.

If you want to get scientific about color mixing, make yourself color samples around the color wheel. A cardboard color wheel can usually be bought from an art supply store or online as a guide to color mixing. I prefer the Ives color wheel, but almost any of them will be of great help for you. By varying the amount of each of two primary colors that you add to each other, you can create all of the colors in between the two primaries. For example, between yellow and blue you get a range of blue-green, apple green, avocado, and greenish yellows.

Create one bead from each of the colors that can be made using a specific pair of primary colors, and then string them in the order in which they were created. This can be done with each pair of primaries. Keeping notes on which primaries you used and the amounts you mixed will ensure that later you can repeat any of the colors you want. Two primaries mixed together yield a secondary color. Red and yellow make orange. Blue and yellow make green. Blue and red make purple.

Try mixing two secondary colors to see what they yield also. Try adding increasing amounts of white to a color, and keep a record of that. Adding white to a color makes lighter colors (tints) with the same hue. Adding black or umber makes darker colors (shades). There are many ways to increase your color vocabulary.

Note: See the Techniques section of the book for a special color mixing technique called the Skinner blend.

Your Own Color Palette

Once you feel easy with mixing, then it's time to see if you can find your own personal color palette. Take a look around at the natural world. During the summer, colors are more dynamic and pure. Spring colors are softer and more fragile, just tints of summer colors. Autumn's hues are rich and warm, while winter colors are the most understated. Try to determine which of these you prefer. Or maybe you are like me. I love all the seasons and move from one palette to another, depending on my mood. What matters is that you work with a palette that you enjoy.

Try to find classes in color theory in your area. In addition, there are many books on the subject. With some study and experimentation, you will soon find that working with color will become easy.

15. Color wheels of clay beads, made by mixing colors, can be reference samples for future work.

Some Basic Techniques

In order to avoid repeating the instructions for certain techniques over and over again with each project, I have put many of them into the following section so that you can refer to them whenever you need to. In some projects, however, you will find less common or even brand-new techniques, which are explained with the project. A few extra techniques are included here too, even though they are not used in the projects, because they offer you opportunities to try new directions for your work. Where a specific brand is mentioned, it usually means that only that brand of paper, leafing pen, etc., works for the technique, as of this writing, or that I have found it to work best.

images from rubber stamps, books, and other sources; then cannibalize them by cutting out portions and recombining them into your own art.

So now you have the images. How do you turn them into rubber stamps? It's easy and fairly inexpensive. First, arrange as many images as you can get inside a 9" × 7" (22 × 18 cm) space on a white piece of paper. This is your camera-ready art. Next, find one of the rubber stamp suppliers that specialize in making these types of stamps and send off your artwork. As a rule, you will get back 3 things: a sheet of rubber stamps, which can be cut apart and mounted onto wood or baked clay; a sheet of rigid plastic that is the same as the rubber stamps, except that it tends to work better when impressing the clay; and a matrix board that is actually a mold of the rubber stamps.

1 RUBBER STAMPS AND CLAY STAMPS

Rubber stamps are great tools to use with clay. However, not all rubber stamps are equal. Stamps that are cut too shallow do not give much of an impression. Be sure to check how deeply the rubber is cut when you buy them. What you want are nice, straight sides and edges. If they are rounded, they will not work well. The harder the rubber, the better. Acrylic stamps are even better than rubber, but these usually must be custom-made and are quite expensive. Soft, spongy material makes for soft, diffuse impressions.

Think about size and detail and make sure your stamps are suited for use with the clay. Huge, bold stamps may not give you the look you want, and very finely detailed ones may not show up as much as you'd like. It won't take you long to learn which ones are the most effective.

Making Rubber Stamps

Your own art can be reborn as a rubber stamp very easily. For this your art must be a black-and-white line drawing (no gray tones). Check out the copyright-free graphics that come with many computer programs or are found in a variety of books. Size them up or down to suit your needs.

You can create "original" art for rubber stamps by using a collage method. Collect a wide variety of printed

How to Use Your Rubber Stamps

1. Before using your stamp to impress a design into the clay, use some type of release medium so that the clay doesn't stick to the rubber; Armorall™ (the stuff used for polishing the interior of automobiles), cornstarch, talc, and even plain water can be used.
2. If you are using talc or cornstarch, it is a good idea to make a pounce bag. Simply cut out a square of cotton fabric, pour a good amount of the powder into the center, bundle up the edges, and then tie them together with a cord. Then all you have to do is to "pounce" the bottom of the bag: tap it against the surface you want to protect. Some of the powder will filter through the fabric in just the right amount.
3. When you are ready to impress the clay with the stamp, set the stamp on your work surface with the rubber side up, and lay the clay over it. Begin pushing down on the clay with your fingers or palms, making certain that it goes into all of the recessed areas.
4. Gently peel the clay away from the stamp.
5. If you want to have designs on both sides of the clay, sandwich the clay between two rubber stamps and press

together. Some clay artists stand on top of the stamp for added pressure. But be cautious, as some thin pieces of clay can be cut through by pressing too hard.

6. Another way to use rubber stamps is to ink them as you would when stamping on paper and then press them into the raw clay. This will leave a nicely colored impression. The ink acts as a release. Or use an inked stamp on a flat piece of baked clay.

7. If you use a pigment type of ink, you should rebake the piece for a short time, or use a heat gun to set the ink.

8. You can also use mica powders to color stamped areas. Just press the stamp into the mica powder and then stamp into the raw clay.

1. Pushing clay into a stamp and lifting the clay.

2. The resulting piece of raw clay, with cornstarch on it.

Clay Stamps

You can make impression stamps out of polymer clay.

1. Use a carving tool to incise the design you want into the clay, before or after baking.

2. Bake these stamps for at least an hour at the clay manufacturer's recommended temperature to assure that they are sturdy.

3. Spray all of your impression stamps with Armorall, or dust them with talc or cornstarch before using so they don't stick to the unbaked clay.

2 MOLDS & TEXTURE SHEETS

Commercial Molds

A number of commercial molds made just for use with polymer clay are available, including ones that have a stamp on one side and a mold of that stamp on the other. Some are wonderfully flexible. You can also use candy or food molds (but don't use them for food after that). Commercial molds do not always have the type of image you are looking for, which can be frustrating. The answer is to make your own molds.

Making Molds

Super Elasticlay Molds

Polyform makes a flexible clay called Super Elasticlay that works very well for making molds as well as flexible strings of clay for weaving and crocheting. Super Elasticlay is a favorite of many clayers.

1. Knead the Elasticlay to prepare for use.

2. Take your original object that you want to mold, and cover it with a mold release, such as cornstarch, including the edges.

3. Press the object into a lump of Elasticlay the same size as the object or a little bigger, which you have secured to your work surface.

4. If the object you are molding will melt in baking, remove it from the mold by pulling it gently away. If

1. Molded clay pieces and the molds they came from. At upper left, a few more molds.

you don't get a good image, you can just wad it up and try again. It won't harden until it's baked.

5. Bake according to the package directions; don't overbake.

6. When you use your Elasticlay molds, use a separator such as cornstarch to keep the polymer clay from sticking to the mold.

Easy Molding with Two-Part Molding Material

Many clay artists began by making molds of leftover waste polymer clay, which works very well and is easy to do. Many still use this method at times. However, the desire for a mold that is flexible has finally resulted in the invention of new materials.

There are now a variety of two-part molding materials. In a matter of minutes, with no baking, you can make a mold of just about anything. These molds are soft and flexible, allowing for a certain amount of undercuts. You never need to use a mold release with them, which is great. It is even possible to make a double-sided mold by covering the entire object with the mold material, letting it set up, and then slicing it in half with a craft knife. Some of these molding materials are silicone-based, like those used for casting for hearing aids, while others have a different formula, but all of them work extremely well.

You will need two-part molding material in an amount that is sufficient for the item you wish to mold. The material is sold by the jar or in pre-measured single-use packs. Some excellent ones are: Puffinalia Miracle Mold, Polymer Clay Express Molding compound, and Mega-Sil from Microsonic, the same material used to form perfect molds of the inside of a person's ear.

■ 1. Choosing Items to Mold with Two-Part Molding Material

Almost any item can be molded; however not every item may make a useful mold. Consider the size of the item you wish to mold. Very large items will take a large amount of mold material. Look for items that have many two-dimensional details. Sculpted bas-relief images make excellent molds.

If you can sculpt, you may want to make a mold of your creation, so that you can replicate it without having to go through the entire process of sculpting each time you wish to make one.

For molds for embellishing your work, choose items to mold that are highly detailed and have depressions that are deep, for example:

❖ Earrings that have an interesting surface
❖ A portion of a segmented bracelet
❖ Highly decorative buttons
❖ Faceted plastic or glass gems
❖ Filigree pieces, either metal or plastic
❖ Carved bone pieces

Deeply cut rubber stamps can also be molded, but please note that some stamp companies do not allow you to use their stamps in any way except for stamping. Check with them if you intend to use the stamps in other ways and plan to sell the work made with them.

■ 2. *Making the Mold with Two-Part Molding Material*

These are general instructions. Follow the package instructions for the specific molding compound you choose.

❖ Choose the object you wish to mold.
❖ Measure out equal parts of the molding material (silicone + catalyst or whatever the two parts are).
❖ Quickly and briskly mix the two together for about 20 seconds. Roll the molding material into a ball, and then flatten it slightly into a fat patty.
❖ If the object that you are going to mold has a fairly flat bottom, set it down onto your work surface and then lay the molding material on top; press down on the molding material gently to force the material into the depressions. Do not move the material back and forth sideways, as this will distort the image or cause a ghost. Just press down and then press in a little from the sides.
❖ If the back of the object to be molded is not fairly flat, lay the piece of molding material down on your work surface, place the object to be molded on top, impression-side down, and press the piece into the

material. Press just until the back of the piece is flush with the top of the molding material. Press in on the sides lightly.

❖ Work fast, as the mold material will begin to set up very quickly. It will become firm yet flexible in a matter of minutes.
❖ Once the mold is firm, gently pop the object from the mold. Let the mold sit for another 10 minutes before using. It should now be completely cured and stable.
❖ If it should ever rip or tear, simply use more uncured molding material on the outside to fix it.

■ 3. *Choosing Clay for Molding with Flexible Molds*

❖ Firm clay can be removed from a flexible mold with little if any distortion.
❖ Soft clay will distort a great deal when you try to move it out of undercuts in the mold, as the mold material is flexible. The resulting image sometimes is not as clearly detailed as it would be with firmer clay. If your clay is extremely soft, you can either leach it or cool it in the refrigerator.
❖ Leaching consists of removing the excess plasticizer by putting the conditioned clay between some sheets of plain paper. When the paper looks oily, it means some of the plasticizer from the clay is being absorbed. This will make the clay less soft. Don't use paper with ink on it, as it will pick up the ink. Check periodically to see if the clay has become firm enough.
❖ Leaching and cooling will both improve the quality of the molded image. If your piece has some undercuts and you are working with soft clay, be sure to use one of these methods to firm it up before molding.

■ 4. *Using the Flexible Mold*

❖ Condition a piece of clay about the size that will fit into the mold.
❖ Hold the mold in one hand to support it, and press the clay into it with the other. Press it in well, working all around the top edges of the clay so that it doesn't overlap the top surface of the mold.

❖ If there is still an excess of clay on the top, slice it off with a sharp blade. Be careful when doing this, as the blade can easily cut into the mold material.

❖ Once you have done this, simply flex the mold all around, and pop out the molded piece. You should never need to use a mold release such as talc with a flexible mold made of 2-part molding material. You can mold another piece immediately in the same mold, without any sticking.

❖ It is possible to bake your clay inside one of these molds. Most silicones can tolerate the amount of heat needed to bake the clay. The advantage of baking in the mold is that there is no possibility of misshaping a raw piece of clay while trying to remove it from the mold.

Texture Sheets and Other Tools

There are various types of texture sheets that you can use with the clay. Clear plastic sheets, thin unmounted rubber stamps, etched copper plates, and thin polymer clay sheets will all work. All of them need some kind of release medium so that the clay does not stick to the sheets. From my experience, plain water is the easiest and least messy to use. Some people prefer to use cornstarch or Armorall; however, these tend to build up in the texture sheets when they mix with the ingredients in the clay.

To use water, simply fill a small spray bottle and spritz it onto the surface of the sheet, shake off the excess, and then place the clay against the wet side of the sheet. Run the two through the pasta machine; the clay will be very easy to remove.

You can also use sheets of textured fabric with the clay, but for these it is best to use a cornstarch release. I have had fairly good luck using wet fabric, but the depth of the texturing is somewhat shallow. Experiment with this to see how it works for you.

Once you look around you will see that hundreds of things will serve as tools for texturing clay, including narrow tubes, combs, brushes, plastic needlepoint canvases, and screwdrivers.

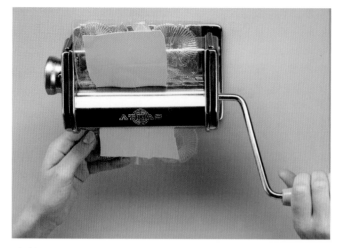

2. Using a texture sheet in a pasta machine.

3. Impressing clay with a narrow tube. On table, some examples of textured clay and texture tools.

4. Texturing with another texture tool.

3 IMAGE TRANSFERS

One of the wonderful things about polymer clay is its ability to grab an image such as a copy of a photograph, a graphic, or a piece of artwork, and hang onto it. Using the following techniques, you can add images to just about anything you wish to make.

1. King's Ransom, black-and-white toner transfer by Dotty McMillan.

Black-and-White Transfers Onto Raw Clay (5-Minute Transfer)

Many methods of doing black-and-white transfers have been developed. I prefer the fast and easy method that I call my 5-minute transfer technique, given below. I've found it almost fail-safe. This method gives you a reversed image, so if you have type in it or if the direction of the image is important, reverse your image first.

1. For the best image, use a fairly fresh copy-shop copy from a machine that uses toner or a copy from a laser printer. After a month or so, the toner seems to degrade or harden, and your image will not be as good as it should be, or it may not transfer at all.

2. Prepare a piece of clay of the size and shape you want. This should be a smooth, flat, light-colored or white piece of clay. Lay the clay on whatever baking surface you will be using. This step is very important.

3. Cut out your transfer picture from its paper and lay it face down on the clay surface.

4. Burnish the back of the paper well, rubbing the paper with a smooth, hard object such as a bone folder, paper-embossing burnishing tool, a tongue depressor, or the dull edge of a dinner knife. Rub hard enough to assure that the paper is well seated on the clay, but not so hard that you dig into the clay. Burnish the surface at least 3 or 4 times (Photo 2). Don't remove the paper.

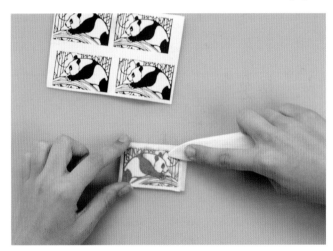

2. Burnishing an image onto clay with a bone folder.

5. Place the clay on its baking surface in a preheated oven. Use an oven thermometer to get exactly the temperature that has been recommended by the clay manufacturer. DO NOT pick up the clay from the baking surface, as this can dislodge the paper. Any area of the image that does not touch the clay during baking will not transfer.

6. Bake the piece for 5 minutes with the paper in place. Remove the piece from the oven and slowly and carefully lift off the paper (Photo 3). Return the clay to the oven and continue baking for the rest of the required time for that kind/thickness of clay. It should give you a nice sharp, dark transfer.

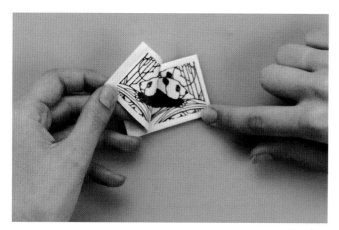

3. The transferred, reversed image.

Black-and-White Transfers with Colored Pencils

This technique is exactly the same as the regular black-and-white transfer just described, except for one step: Before cutting out your black-and-white image, color it with colored pencils. Make sure that you exert enough pressure to coat the paper well with color, so that it will transfer well. Different brands of colored pencils and certain colors create different effects. Do some testing before you begin a project so that you won't be disappointed in the results.

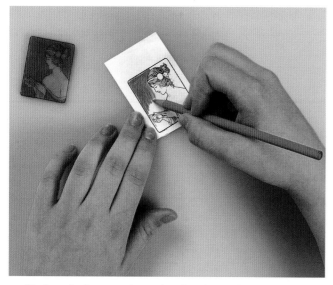

4. Black-and-white transfer with colored pencils. At right, coloring in an image; left, the finished image on translucent clay.

Black-and-White Transfers with Colored Pencils on Translucent Clay, Backed with Metallic Foils

5. Geisha is made with a black-and-white transfer, colored pencils, and gold leaf. By Dotty McMillan.

This is a technique that has beautiful results.

1. What you need is a very, very thin piece of translucent clay. This can be achieved by placing a sheet of translucent clay rolled on the #4 setting (⁵⁄₆₄" or 1.6 mm) of the pasta machine between the halves of a folded piece of waxed paper and running it through the pasta machine. Then open up the paper, loosen the clay from it, and replace it inside the waxed paper. Turn the pasta machine setting to one size thinner and run it through again. Repeat a total of 3 times, or until you reach the #7 setting (¹⁄₄₀" or 0.6 mm) on the pasta machine.

2. Loosen the thin sheet carefully from the waxed paper but place it back down on the waxed paper. Lay the black-and-white transfer that has been colored with pencils face down onto the clay, and burnish the back of the paper well. Lay the top sheet of waxed paper back over the clay and the transfer, and burnish again over the waxed paper. Turn the piece over and burnish the front through the waxed paper. Bake for the recommended time in the waxed paper. Remove the translucent piece and let cool.

3. Once you have baked the translucent piece, you are ready to add the foil. Coat the areas where you wish

ARTFUL WAYS WITH POLYMER CLAY

the foil to be (possibly avoiding faces), with a foil adhesive such as Old World Art Leafing Adhesive, and let dry. Be certain that you coat and leaf the surface of the transferred piece that is holding the color and ink. Lay the piece with the adhesive side down onto a sheet of gold, silver, or copper foil or leaf. Use a small brush to remove any of the foil in areas in which you did not put adhesive.

4. Add a thin coat of liquid clay to the back of the foil; then place the piece with its attached foil on a sheet of white or light-colored clay and trim to the size and shape you want. Bake again.

5. Sand and buff the surface, or finish with 0000 steel wool. If you have put the adhesive and foil on the correct side of the piece, the sanding will not harm the transfer.

Inkjet Color Transfers

Regular paper: Color copies of pictures that are done at a copy shop onto regular paper will transfer onto the raw clay via the same method used for the regular black-and-white transfers (see page 25). However, the image with this type of transfer is often light or pale, although now and then you may get a brighter image, depending on where you have your copy made. Try different copy shops until you find one whose color copies transfer well. (Softer, paler images may be just the effect you want, however.)

Inkjet T-Shirt Transfer Paper: For brightest color, you should use the Lazertran Inkjet paper (see page 31). However, if you are not able to locate this paper in your vicinity and want really bright color transfers, you can use inkjet T-shirt transfer paper manufactured by Canon or Hewlett Packard. These are the only two that I know of at this time that work well, but it is a good idea to experiment, as these types of papers are modified often. You will need a computer, a paint or picture-editing program, and an inkjet printer. If you plan to use photographs or other pictures besides the ones you have on your computer, you will also need access to a scanner.

1. Create or scan in your image and print it on T-shirt transfer paper from an inkjet printer.

2. Follow all of the directions for the 5-minute black-and-white transfer (see page 25), with the exception of the timing. Bake the color transfer with the paper in place for 7 to 10 minutes; remove the piece from the oven and very carefully peel off the paper.

3. Return the piece to the oven and complete the baking time. The transfer paper works because it is coated with a gluelike substance, which melts onto the clay.

4. Sometimes you will notice some waviness or tiny bumps on the surface after the piece is baked. This can't always be avoided. However, you can coat the surface with a very thin layer of Translucent Liquid Sculpey and rebake it. Be sure you coat all the way to the edge of the piece and then on around onto the side edges; otherwise, the liquid clay will tend to peel off.

5. The baked surface can then be sanded and buffed, or left as is. Glazing is also a possibility, using two or more coats of any of the clay-compatible glazes. Or buff the surface with 0000 steel wool for a matte finish.

6. Wheel type kaleidoscope uses Lazertran Inkjet transfers. By Dotty McMillan.

Translucent Liquid Clay Transfers

Another method of doing color transfers is to use liquid clay as an adjunct. Some colored magazine pictures will transfer using the liquid. Once you use the picture, that's it; you can't use it again.

1. Coat a piece of glass or nonporous tile with Translucent Liquid Sculpey or Kato Liquid Polyclay.

2. Cut out the picture and lay it face down on the liquid clay. Bake with the paper in place for the time and temperature recommended by the clay manufacturer.

3. While the piece is still hot, carefully peel off the paper; your image will have been transferred onto the clay.

Other Uses of Liquid Clay with Transfers: Images that have been printed with an inkjet printer onto T-shirt transfer paper can also be transferred using liquid clay in the way described above. A very thin layer of liquid clay applied to polymer clay before the image is burnished on is also helpful to speed up the transfer of black-and-white images and to urge older copies to transfer.

One of the projects in this book (Michelle Ross's Frames project) outlines another interesting way to use liquid clay to transfer images that are printed on an inkjet printer.

Lazertran Papers

During the past few years, special image transfer papers from the Lazertran Company have become available: Lazertran Silk, Regular Lazertran, and Lazertran for Inkjet printers. And no, the first-named paper isn't made out of silk; it was designed to transfer an image onto silk fabric so that it remains soft to the touch and moves with the material.

Lazertran Silk: With Lazertran Silk, you can do perfect transfers of either color images or black-and-white images onto raw clay, which you can then place on a rounded or curved surface (or a flat surface) before baking. Lazertran Silk transfers only the toner powders from the printed image. There are several transfer methods that work well with Lazertran Silk. Two are described in this section. The only drawback is that your image must be printed onto the Lazertran Silk paper using a color photocopier, usually found at a copy shop. The copier must run at or below 356°F (180°C). You cannot use an inkjet printer with the Lazertran Silk type of transfer paper or with Lazertran Regular. Note: A reversed image is produced with Lazertran Silk.

Lazertran Regular is a decal type of transfer that uses a very thin sheet of plastic to hold the toner powders. Images may be used either reversed or not reversed with Lazertran Regular. These decals do not do well when

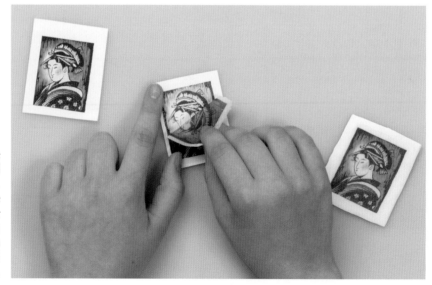

7. Transferring an image with translucent liquid clay. Left: The image. Middle: Peeling off the translucent clay transfer after it is baked. Right: The image backed with white clay. See page 75 for details.

heated, so it is best to use Lazertran Regular on already-baked clay.

Lazertran for Inkjets is also a decal type of transfer. Its advantage is that images can be printed at home using any inkjet printer. Lazertran for Inkjets is used for putting images onto the surface of already-baked clay, not raw clay. A coating of a white craft glue, such as Sobo, on the baked surface will help the Lazertran inkjet decal to adhere.

Consult the Lazertran web site (www.lazertran.com) for details about which copiers can be used and for emerging information.

Note: When choosing background clay colors for your Lazertran transfers, remember that Lazertran Regular and Silk papers will be transparent, and Lazertran Inkjet paper will be semi-transparent. A dark clay background for an image will make it difficult to see. Bright colors will change the color of the image. White and ecru or beige show up the colors of transfers very well. Gold makes for a very soft sepia, antiqued look.

No-Heat Method with Lazertran Silk

1. Have the image you want copied onto the shiny side of Lazertran Silk paper on a color photocopier. Remember to reverse the image if you have type in it, as the final image will be reversed.

2. Cut out the transfer, leaving a thin edge around the image. Roll out a light-colored sheet of clay in a size that will fit your transfer. When finished, the background of the decal will be transparent.

3. Lay the transfer face-down onto the clay. Burnish the back of the paper with a bone folder, spoon, or other implement.

4. Use a brush or cotton swab to soak the back of the transfer with rubbing alcohol. Burnish over the transfer again. Let the paper dry. Repeat soaking the back of the transfer and burnishing a total of 3 times.

5. When the alcohol has dried, use a spray bottle to soak the back of the transfer with water. Spray a second time so that the water puddles.

6. Tap the back of the transfer with your fingers. Wait several minutes. Gently slide the backing paper off the

8. Sepia-toned brooch uses Lazertran Silk images; by Dotty McMillan.

clay. You should have a perfect transfer. Use a soft piece of T-shirt material or a facial tissue to wick up the excess water. Do not press; just barely touch the clay. If you should happen to have a small spot that doesn't transfer, use acrylic paint or Fiesta inks in a matching color to camouflage the area after the piece is baked.

7. Let the transfer piece dry completely. When dry, trim or cut the clay into whatever shape you need with a cutter or a knife. The transfer piece can then be applied to another piece of raw clay, either flat or rounded. To apply a transfer to a rounded or curved surface that has already been baked, coat the back of the transfer piece with a very thin coat of one of the liquid clays, such as Transparent Liquid Sculpey or Kato Liquid Polyclay, before applying it to the baked piece. This will help it adhere.

8. When you bend raw clay, the transfer will sometimes crackle a little. This gives the piece an antique look that I find quite attractive. It doesn't happen all the time; it depends on how steep the rounding of the base piece is. Letting the transferred piece sit for a day before applying it helps diminish the crackling.

9. You can leave the transfer piece just as is when it comes out of the oven after baking. The transfer will hold up very well even with a lot of use. It is usually nice and smooth with a soft sheen to it. However, for more protection, coat the surface of the transfer with one of the clay-compatible glazes.

9. Two pendants made with Lazertran Silk.

10. Evening bag made over large matchbox uses Lazertran Silk images; by Dotty McMillan.

Lazertran Regular Paper

You cannot use Lazertran Regular paper to transfer images onto raw clay. The plastic decal interacts with the clay and becomes extremely sticky. The two actually melt together. This stickiness does not go away after baking. You can use Lazertran Regular paper with already-baked clay. It is quite easy to use, unless you are working with very large transfers. In this case you must be very careful, as the plastic decal loves to wrinkle. You can lift it, however, and place it down again. It is somewhat delicate, but even so it can be handled successfully. It can be placed flat, or put on rounded surfaces and carefully manipulated into place. If you did not reverse your image before printing it, and you want to reverse it, you may reverse the decal itself. This will put the ink side of the decal on the top surface, so it will need a coat of clay-compatible glaze to protect it.

1. Have the image copied onto a sheet of Lazertran Regular paper by a color photocopier at a copy shop; reverse if desired.

2. Cut the transfer to the size you wish, leaving a small edge around the image. Place the transfer into a bowl of water. The piece will curl up at first, then it will relax and begin to straighten out. Remove the piece

11. Sliding off image.

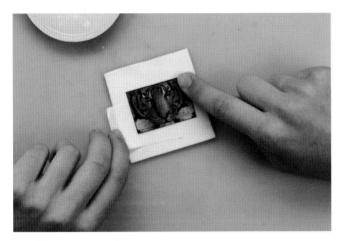

12. Positioning on clay.

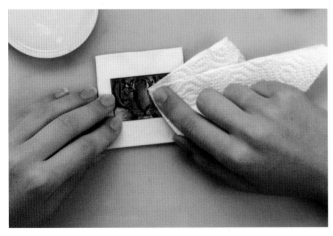

13. Wiping off moisture.

from the water and lay it image-side down onto a paper towel or a piece of newspaper. Blot it with another paper towel to remove excess water.

3. It helps if you first coat the area on the clay piece to which you are transferring the decal with a thin coating of Diamond Flecto Varathane water-based varnish. You must place your transfer on top of the varnish before it dries.

4. To do this, place the image on its paper onto the clay near where you want it. Slide the decal portion out from under the paper backing and onto the piece to which you are transferring it. Pat and move the decal so that it is smooth and in the place where you want it to be. Make sure all the edges are well down. Blot the piece and squeegee the transfer with your fingers to remove any water that may be on or under the surface. If you are adding a decal to a flat piece, you can use a regular squeegee. Let dry. Make sure all the edges of the transfer are down. If not, use a bit of white glue to secure them.

5. You can leave the piece as is or coat the transfer with a clay-compatible glaze. Several coats of Varathane varnish will also hide the edges of the decal.

Lazertran for Inkjet Printers

Lazertran now makes an excellent paper for inkjet printers. Lazertran Inkjet is a waterslide decal type of paper similar to the Lazertran Regular. It is used only for clay pieces that have already been baked. The image you make with Lazertran Inkjet can be used right-side up or reversed, but if it is used with the ink side up, it needs to be glazed on the ink side.

1. Print out your images onto the correct side of Lazertran for Inkjet paper using your inkjet printer, thus avoiding a trip to the copy shop (as well as trying to find a copy shop that will let you use their copier for Lazertran Silk or Regular papers). Use the fast setting on the printer, as the paper can only take on a certain amount of ink or it will tend to bleed. Let the printout dry for an hour. This makes the ink waterproof, in case your printer uses ink that will run when wet.

2. Cut out the image you want and submerge the paper in water for about one minute, or until the decal comes loose from the backing paper.

3. Coat the surface of the baked clay where you plan to put the decal with white craft glue, such as Sobo. Slide the decal onto the wet glue, smooth it, and let dry.

4. A double coat of water-based Varathane varnish will protect the transfer once it is dry.

Note about transparency: The background of a Lazertran Inkjet decal isn't clear; it has a light sepia tone to it. If you wish it to be clear, after printing, let the ink on the transfer paper dry for an hour. Then coat the surface of the transfers with an oil-based Varathane varnish. This will make the background transparent. You can coat an individual transfer or a full page of transfers. Do this before you cut them out and transfer them. Two coats of varnish should do the trick.

Note: There are other brands of transfer papers available, but so far, in testing, I've found that Lazertran works best for me. Lazertran papers are available in most parts of the world. However, if you find another brand, by all means experiment with it and see how it works for you.

Tattoo Paper Transfers with Inkjet Printer

Tattoo papers are decal-type waterslide papers and are used much like the Lazertran Regular paper. Tattoo papers result images that are quite crackled and antique-appearing. They can be bought plain or with images already printed on them. The plain paper can be printed on an inkjet printer. There are various brands of tattoo paper; most can be found at a store that carries a large variety of special papers for computer printers. I won't go into detail here as each of the papers has slightly different instructions on the package, which you should follow. Tattoo transfers may be used on raw or baked clay, but must be protected by a thin layer of translucent clay or liquid clay if you use them on raw clay. On baked clay, protect them with a layer of clay-compatible glaze.

4 SIMPLE SILK-SCREENING

Silk-screening onto the surface of polymer clay is one of the best techniques to be perfected in the past few years. The basic concept of silk-screening is simple. A screen is assembled of fabric that has a weave with very small holes. Frequently there is a frame to hold the fabric. The fabric is coated with a light-sensitive chemical. An image is put on the screen by one of several means. The screen is exposed to light or somehow treated so that it hardens and won't let ink pass through it. The image blocks the light, so those areas where the image is don't harden. The original image is washed away, leaving open screen areas in its place that ink can pass through.

Then some fairly thick ink or paint is spread onto the screen with a squeegee. The places where there is no image do not let the ink go through, but the ink goes through all the image places on the screen. The ink is divided up into an even layer by the small holes of the screen, and is deposited on whatever is under the screen (fabric, polymer clay, a T-shirt, etc.). Originally the fabric used for screens was silk. But silk changes size a lot with the weather. Synthetic fabrics are now used because they are more stable.

14. Silkscreened clock.

You can buy a silk screen at an art supply store and learn how to transfer images. Everyone I know has his or her favorite way of doing this. All seem to give good results. However, new products have made silk-screening very easy. Here is my favorite, using a product called PhotoEZ Stencil™. It's available in most parts of the world by mail order or by ordering online. Look at www.photoezsilkscreen.com or www.photoez.us for more information.

Making the Screen with PhotoEZ Stencil

1. To use PhotoEZ Stencil, you need a good black-and-white image, printed on inexpensive 20-lb computer paper. Print it on the "best" setting. Don't go for heavier paper as it won't give you good results. You could use a sheet of transparency plastic instead if you wish. It's best for you to follow the directions on the PhotoEZ Stencil package, but I'll give a simple outline here so you can see what is involved. Use an opaque pen if you're creating your artwork by hand. Very small images and very thin lines won't work well.

2. If you live where it's sunny most of the time, you will not need any special lights. If you lack sun, you can use a fluorescent lamp of wattage equal to 100 or 200 watts, in a reflector. It's the ultraviolet light that affects the screen.

3. In addition to your image, you need a smooth board, a sheet of fairly heavy glass or plastic, a piece of PhotoEZ Stencil screen, a squeegee, and some acrylic paint. The screen is light-sensitive and should remain in a lightproof package until it's used. It has a shelf life of 6 months to a year. The coating on the screen is water-soluble until exposed to light.

4. Work in subdued light. Cut a piece of PhotoEZ to the size you need, leaving a border of at least ½" around your artwork. Remove the plastic backing from the screen. Then set the screen on the board, place the black-and-white image face down onto the screen, and add the sheet of glass on top of the screen. Use clips such as bulldog clips to hold the screen, board, paper, and glass tightly together.

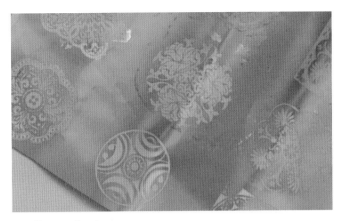

15. Screen detail.

5. If you are using sunlight to expose the screen, take the whole assembly outside and set it so that the sun hits the entire assembly through the glass. Leave it for the time suggested on the stencil package. Usually for computer paper it takes about 5 minutes; for a transparency, about 1 minute. If you are using fluorescent light it takes longer, perhaps from 20 minutes to an hour, depending on the light and the thickness of the paper.

6. After the time is up, remove the screen and place it in a sink or bowl of tap water. Let it sit for 5 or 10 minutes. Rinse the screen under slowly running water to help wash away the residue of screen in the image area. Where the image blocked the light from going through, the layer underneath on the screen wasn't exposed, and so didn't become waterproof and can be washed away. Your original image appears reversed on the screen, including any type that is there. After exposure to the light, the rest of the screen has become stable. Use a very soft brush to remove any excess screen residue. The remaining screen will be stable but soft and somewhat delicate, so handle with care.

7. Place the screen shiny-side up (you see the mirror image) on paper towels and gently blot up the excess water on the screen with a paper towel; let it air-dry completely.

8. Reexpose the screen to a light source to harden for at least 10 minutes more.

Using Silk Screens with the Clay

1. Now you have your screen. You need to use a flat layer of clay to accept the image. It can be shaped later. Lay out the raw clay on your work surface. Place the screen with the shiny side down onto the clay. The image is now not reversed. Smooth out the screen with your hand to make sure it is well positioned against the clay.

2. Squeeze out a line of paint across the top edge of the stencil, out of the image area. Pull the paint down over the entire stencil, using a squeegee or an old credit card. Run the squeegee back up over the image, distributing the paint well.

3. Then carefully peel the screen off the clay, starting at one end. Place the screen into water immediately to rinse it off, as the paint dries fast. Let the silk-screened surface of your clay dry well before moving it.

4. Lifting the screen to show the silk-screened clay. At left, other examples of silk-screened clay.

Other Types of Silk Screens

Print Gocco screen kits (from RISO, Incorporated) also make screens that will work with polymer clay. These screens are made using cardboard frames, which should be removed after the screen is burned. Without the frame, the screen will cling to the clay, which helps to avoid the situation where the paint runs underneath the screen. More information is at www.gocco.com.

It's also possible to use a thermograph machine to make a screen; it works well but is rather expensive and isn't very mobile.

2. Using a silk screen with acrylic paint.

5 THE SKINNER BLEND

I was fortunate enough to be at The Clay Factory in Escondido, California, when polymer clay artist Judith Skinner was busy mixing and blending all sorts of colors of polymer clay. She began laying out beautiful sheets of clay, which started with one color on one side and then blended into a second color on the other. I couldn't believe my eyes! She was easily doing something that most of us had done in a zillion tedious steps. She was developing a fantastic and innovative

3. Spreading the paint with a squeegee.

new technique, later named the Skinner blend after its creator. You will find dozens of uses for Skinner blends. Here's what to do to make one.

Before you start, consider the colors. Some colors blend beautifully, some don't. If you incorporate clays that have all 3 primaries (red, yellow, and blue), the blended color in the center of the sheet of clay sometimes becomes muddy. However, at other times the result can be incredibly beautiful. (Keep a record of what colors you use so that you can repeat the effect later on.) Beautiful shaded blends can be made using just one color with white. Instead of white, try metallic silver or ecru/beige, which will mute the main color and give it a much different look. It's possible to blend more than two colors, and you can even achieve a beautiful rainbow effect. Translucent colors make lovely blends also, as do the pearl colors. The following is a description of a Skinner blend using two colors:

1. Once you have chosen the two colors, roll out a rectangular sheet of each on the #1 setting (⅛" or 3.2 mm) of the pasta machine. These sheets should be just as wide as the pasta machine. Cut each sheet diagonally into 2 triangles. Stack the like-colored triangles together (for example, yellow on yellow and blue on blue). Each double-thick triangle will become one-half of a rectangle (Photo 1). Fit the two different-colored triangles back into a rectangle, butting the edges together firmly.

2. Fold the rectangle in half, from the bottom up (Photo 2). Place the folded edge in the pasta machine and run it through on the thickest setting (Photo 3). Fold the rectangle again, exactly the same way as you did before, from the bottom up. Do not change directions and fold from another side, as this will ruin your blend. Run the clay through the pasta machine again.

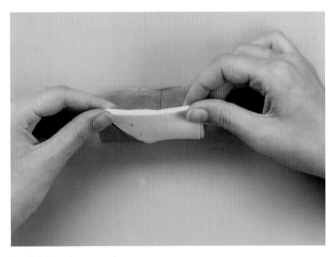

2. Folding the triangles.

3. Starting to blend the clay with the pasta machine.

1. The two triangles of clay.

3. Continue folding and running the clay through about 20 times, or until the color blend is nice and smooth (Photo 4).

4. Now turn your sheet sideways and run it through the pasta machine on the second-thickest setting (⁷⁄₆₄" or 2.8 mm). Do not fold it. If the piece is too wide across when turned this way to fit in the machine, cut it down the middle and stack the two pieces together.

5. Roll the piece through the machine a second time on a setting that is two levels thinner than the last one, and repeat this process until you reach the thinnest setting that you can use without the clay shredding or sticking to the rollers. For some machines this will be a #5 setting (¹⁄₁₆" or 1.6 mm). For others it may be a #6 or #7 (¹⁄₃₂" or ¹⁄₄₀"; 0.8 or 0.6 mm). Some machines have the widths numbered in reverse, so do what will achieve the desired thickness on your particular machine. You will end up with a very long, very thin sheet of clay that should blend from one color at one end to the second color at the other end.

6. Now you have some choices. You can roll this long sheet into a log (to make a blended cane), starting at either end of the sheet. Or fold the long sheet back and forth, accordion style, to make a blended loaf. Try cut-

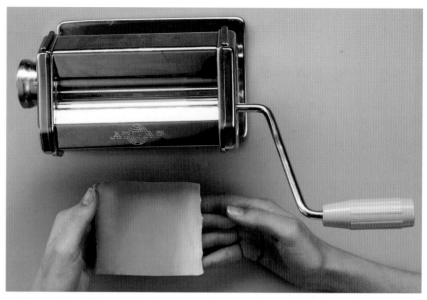

4. The resulting Skinner blend.

ting and stacking pieces so that one color is at one end and the other color is at the other end. Once your log or loaf is finished, you can use it for all sorts of projects. For example, a shaded log works very well when making the petals for flower canes or when making leaf canes. It gives an illusion of dimension.

There are several other ways to do a Skinner blend, placing the triangles differently (see Photo 5 for one example). You will find these demonstrated on a number of polymer clay videotapes.

5. Another Skinner blend with different colors and clay arrangement.

6 MOKUME GANE

This unusual polymer clay technique has been adapted from an ancient Japanese metal-working version. Polymer clay is wonderfully suited for this multilayered technique. There are several ways of achieving mokume gane's lovely effects, all of which work extremely well. See which of them works best for your projects. Translucent clay and metallic leaf are the main ingredients of some but not all of the mokume gane techniques.

Below I have included a rundown on a number of different mokume techniques, which can be used in the projects in this book or for other projects.

1. Four pod beads include two using mokume gane techniques.

Topographical Mokume Gane

1. Roll out a number of balls of translucent clay, each about the size of a walnut. Tint each ball a different color or shade with your choice of opaque clay. Add only a tiny amount of the opaque color to the translucent clay.

2. Flatten each ball and run it through the pasta machine on the #4 (⁵⁄₆₄" or 2 mm) or #5 (¹⁄₁₆" or 1.6 mm) setting. You want each sheet to be quite thin. Cut the sheets into squares about 3" × 3" (7.5 × 7.5 cm).

3. Layer as follows: Lay down a translucent sheet of clay, then a sheet of gold leaf (or other color leaf) on top of it, then a translucent sheet of clay. Repeat until you have a stack that is about 1" to 2" (2.5 to 5 cm) tall.

4. Roll 6 to 8 balls of tinted translucent clay that are a little larger than peas. Turn over the pad of stacked clay and metallic leaf, and place the balls randomly over the bottom surface of the pad. Leave some space between them. Press them lightly to adhere them to the surface (Photo 2).

5. Turn the pad over again, and set it on your work surface. Press down around each of the balls of clay. Do not press the balls themselves, just the spaces between them.

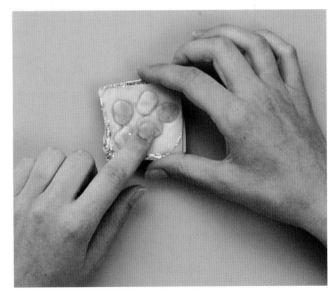

2. Topographical mokume gane: view of the underside of the clay pad.

6. Press your mokume pad against the work surface to anchor it somewhat so that when you are taking slices from it, it won't move. Using a very sharp, thin blade held horizontally with the sharp edge toward you, take extremely thin slices across the tops or domes of clay on your clay pad. Lay these slices on a piece of waxed paper (Photo 3). Take as many slices as your stack of clay will allow. Your finished clay pad should look somewhat like a 3-D topographical map. Use your mokume gane slices for a wide variety of projects, including beads and precious pods. The leftover portion of your pad can also be used, perhaps for a pin and earrings.

4. Impressed-from-top mokume gane; using texture tools to prepare the pad prior to slicing.

3. Once you have finished impressing the clay, secure it to your work surface and begin taking the same kind of thin slices from the stacked pad (Photo 5) as you did with the topographical pad. Set the slices aside to use on clay projects.

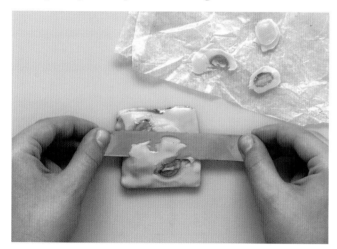

3. Slicing off pieces for topographical mokume gane.

Impressed-from-the-Top Mokume Gane

1. This method starts out exactly the same as the topographical version, as far as making the layers goes (Steps 1 to 3), although you may want to add a layer of opaque clay here and there in your stack. (Don't add the balls of clay below, however.)

2. Once your stack is completed, begin looking around the house and/or a hardware store for various items that you can use to press into the clay to texture it. Make these impressions into the top surface of the stack. Some things that work fairly well are: a large Phillips screwdriver, a zigzag blade, plastic protectors for the bottoms of narrow-legged chairs, a dinner knife to make Xs or squares with, and a corkscrew laid on its side (Photo 4).

5. Taking slices from an impressed mokume gane pad.

A Variation on the Impressed-from-Top Method of Mokume Gane

1. Before impressing, lay on a piece of black or another color of clay as the top layer of the clay pad.
2. When the clay is impressed from above, the black clay will move downward for several layers, outlining the impression images. Black makes the most visible outlines, but other colors can also be used.

6. Precious pod made with impressed-from-top mokume gane technique.

Impressed Slice-Off Mokume Gane

This is actually the reverse of most of the other methods. Instead of taking slices and using the slices to lay onto another base clay to decorate it, in this method you impress the clay with rubber stamps and then remove very thin slices of the raised areas, which reveals the colors and patterns of clay underneath. It is the underneath portion that you use to make pins and pendants, to cover vessels, and so forth.

1. Roll out sheets of clay in 3 different colors on the #1 setting (⅛" or 3.2 mm) of the pasta machine. Stack the colors together.
2. Roll the stack through the pasta machine just once on the #1 setting. Cut the sheet in half and stack again. Roll it through the pasta machine again on the same setting. Repeat one more time. This should give you 12 layers of the different colors of clay.
3. Use a rubber stamp or a mold made from a rubber stamp to press down and make fairly deep impressions in the clay.
4. Anchor your clay to your work surface so that it doesn't slip or slide when you are slicing. Using a tissue

blade or other very sharp and flexible blade, begin taking extremely thin slices off the tops of the raised surfaces. Be careful not to cut too deep, as you will eradicate your pattern. As you slice, you will begin to see the pattern and colors emerge from under the top layer of clay. The resulting piece can then be used for many different projects. This form of mokume looks beautiful when lightly sanded and buffed.

Dragon Skin Mokume Gane

This technique is a mini-form of the impressed slice-off type mokume gane; it gives surprising results. It can be done with a variety of texture sheets, but the ones I like best make a sheet of clay that somewhat resembles a form of reptile skin. Since it can be made in a wide variety of color combinations, it usually resembles my fantasy of a dragon's skin. You will end up using the shaved sheet of clay that remains, not the pieces being shaved away. (However, the tiny shaved-off pieces can be used for small projects such as beads.)

You will need 3 colors of clay, one light, one dark, and one in between. You will also need a plastic texture sheet that has a grid of small dots. Many other sheets will give you interesting effects too, as a little experimenting will soon show you. My favorites are "Dots in a Grid" and one that resembles an array of small fans (see page 40 for using needlepoint canvas).

1. Condition the clay and then roll out a sheet of each color on the widest setting of the pasta machine (⅛" or 3.2 mm). Trim the clay sheets to make rectangles of each color that are about 3" (7.5 cm) wide and 4" (10 cm) long.
2. Place the dark clay on your work surface and place the light clay on top of it. Place the medium-colored clay on top of the light clay. Press or roll over the surface of these 3 stacked sheets of clay to make sure there is no air trapped between them.
3. Set your pasta machine to the widest setting. Roll the stack of sheets lengthwise through the machine. Cut this long sheet of clay in half and stack. Roll it through the pasta machine. Cut, stack, and roll. Repeat this one more time (3 times altogether). Cut the sheet in half and set one piece aside.

4. Spray the concave side (the side where the little rounded areas are indented) of the texture sheet with water. Place the dark side of one of the clay sheets against the sprayed side of the texture sheet. Run the texture sheet and clay through the pasta machine on the widest setting, with the clay side away from you.

5. Carefully peel the clay away from the texture sheet and lay it with textured side up on your work surface. Press the top corners and edges of the sheet firmly against the work surface so that the piece does not move.

6. Holding your tissue blade at each side, lay it parallel with the surface of the clay sheet. Bend it slightly upward. Slice off a very thin layer from the top surface of the textured clay (Photo 7). Continue doing this until the entire surface of the sheet has been shaved. If you feel your blade dig too deeply into the clay, back it off, press the divot back down, and then slice less deeply.

7. Once you have completed the first clay sheet, repeat exactly the same process with the other half that you set aside before, only this time place the opposite (light) side of the clay against the texture sheet instead of the dark side. Once you have shaved off a very thin layer of clay from the second sheet, you will see how different the two halves look. You now have two different looks, but in the same color tones.

7. Slicing off the top layer of the clay. On table, examples of dragon skin mokume gane.

Note: A sheet of plastic needlepoint canvas can also be used instead of a texture sheet. It is used the same way as the texture sheet, except that you must powder both sides of the clay well and also powder the canvas on both sides with cornstarch. The square holes in the canvas are quite deep, and the clay will stick if it is not powdered extremely well. Carefully and slowly peel the clay from the canvas after running it through the pasta machine, and then follow the steps given above.

8. Dragon Skin Treasure Box is an example of the dragon skin technique.

7 CREATING CANES

Cane Basics

Polymer clay has the remarkable ability to be assembled into colorful canes, which can be reduced in size and extruded, and then sliced. The process is basically the making of a three-dimensional design whose cross-section forms an image or pattern. The resulting cane has the same pattern on each cross-sectional slice that is taken from it.

There are really only four substances with which you can make highly detailed canes: glass, candy, cookies, and polymer clay. Cane work is often referred to as millefiori, or "a thousand flowers," a concept derived from Italian glasswork, as well as from glasswork done in ancient Egypt. It is the remarkable ability to be caned, reduced, and extruded that sets polymer clay apart from most other artist's mediums. There are thousands of designs that can be made into canes, including, but certainly not limited to, faces, people, animals, landscapes, geometric patterns, and florals.

To build a cane, make a series of logs or snakes, triangular prisms, rectangular solids, or any of a variety of other shapes and then combine them together in a bundle that forms a picture or design when seen at the ends of the cane. It can be an extremely fat bundle or a

1. Sampler of various canes, including face canes.

thin one. The bundle can be round or square. Photos 2a and b show the start of a round cane. Other shapes besides round and square ones can be made, but they are much harder to reduce to the size you will need.

The term "reduce" means that the cane is rolled, pressed, squeezed, and stretched so that it becomes smaller around and longer. It is possible to reduce a

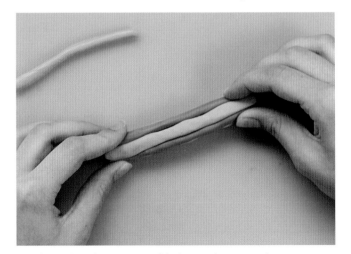

2a. Several snakes are assembled to make a round cane.

2b. The snakes will be rolled farther to reduce them and to join the parts.

cane that starts out with the diameter of a dinner plate all the way down to the diameter of a tiny button and still have whatever pattern you have built into it visible. I do not, however, recommend starting out with a dinner-plate size! A good size to begin with is a cane that is the diameter of a soda can or smaller.

Note: Cane-making with soft clay can make both building the cane and slicing it rather difficult. (See the section about clays for recommendations of clays that are good for canes.) Cane-making with soft clays can be made easier by leaching out some of the chemicals in the clay prior to use.

To leach the clay, roll the clay into a sheet, place it between several pieces of blank computer paper, and rest a heavy object on top. Let it sit overnight, change the paper, and repeat. The excess plasticizer from the clay will be absorbed by the paper. You could also let the cane sit for several days after making it, and/or cool the cane before reducing it and again before slicing.

Reducing Canes

Every clay artist has his or her own favorite way of reducing a cane. The main objective is to reduce your cane to a usable size without distorting the pattern inside and with little waste clay at the ends.

Round Cane

1. Begin squeezing the cane close to one end, turning it around in your fingers so that all of the cane in that area is squeezed equally.
2. Move to the other end and squeeze the same way. Move back and forth between the ends until the cane is equally small in both those areas. The center of the cane will be much fatter. Reduce the ends only until their diameter is about the size that you may want for your first slices.
3. Then begin squeezing the center of the cane, turning it around in your fingers so that there is equal pressure over the entire surface. Once the center is reduced to the same size as the ends, you can continue reducing by rolling the cane on the work surface, using the flat of your hands, pulling outward slightly as you roll.

Plexiglas™ Method

Another technique that many people swear by uses a piece of Plexiglas on each end of a round cane.
1. Slice off each end of the cane so that it is perfectly flat; then place a piece of Plexiglas on each end.
2. Begin the reduction in the middle of the cane, forming a barbell or hourglass shape with the clay. Move outward, reducing toward the ends. The Plexiglas will create suction, which will help to keep the center of the cane from pulling inward, and thus will reduce the amount of cane loss.

Square or Rectangular Cane

1. Set the cane upright and cup it with both hands. Use the heels of your hands to press in on opposite sides. Rotate the cane and press inward again on the next two sides.
2. Flip the cane over, bottom side up, and repeat the pressing.
3. Continue alternating the sides and the pressing until your cane is too long to handle well this way. Then lay the cane down on its side and begin rolling over the sides with a brayer or an acrylic roller. Roll a side, turn the piece one turn, and roll again. Continue this until your cane is the size you desire. It helps if you pick the cane up in your hands now and then and stretch it slightly, smoothing the sides with your fingers; then continue with the rolling.

Jelly Roll Cane

1. Choose two contrasting colors of clay. To form the cane, roll out two 3" × 5" (7.5 × 12.5 cm) sheets of clay, one of each color, on the #1 setting (⅛" or 3.2 mm) of the pasta machine. Lay one sheet on top of the other. Decide which color you wish to dominate. That color should be underneath so it will be on the outside of the roll.
2. Taper the ends of the sheets and then begin to roll up, making sure no air is trapped while doing this (Photo 3). When they are completely rolled, smooth the ends.
3. Reduce the cane by rolling it on your work surface with the palms of your hands, gently pulling outward as you roll. When the length of the piece has doubled,

3. Rolling a jelly roll cane (in hands); on table; loaf and bull's-eye canes.

cut it in half and put one-half away for use later. Continue to reduce the other piece until it is the size you need. Let the cane sit as long as possible before using it so that it firms up throughout. You can then make slices from it that will look like spirals.

Note: See the Tall Teapot project for double jellyroll canes.

Bull's-Eye Cane

These can be used for many things, including making hair, clothing, and eyes for cane faces.
1. Choose one light color and one darker color, such as the black and white used in Photo 3 and 4. Roll out both colors into logs that are about 3" (7.5 cm) long and ½" (1.3 cm) in diameter.
2. Also roll out a sheet of each color on the #4 setting (⁵⁄₆₄" or 2 mm) of the pasta machine; each sheet should be large enough to wrap around a log.
3. Wrap each log with the sheet of the opposite color—white around black, and black around white. Roll both canes smooth.

4. Bull's-eye canes in black and white.

4. Reduce canes as described above for round canes. You now have two bull's-eye canes made of the same colors, but they look different from each other.

Loaf Cane

Narrow strips of a loaf cane can be used to make hair that is standing on end, as well as striped clothing. Loaf canes can also decorate containers (see the Tall Teapot project) and many other things.
1. Choose contrasting colors and roll each out into a sheet on the # 3 (³⁄₃₂" or 2.4 mm) or #4 (⁵⁄₆₄" or 2 mm) setting of the pasta machine.
2. Cut each sheet into a square that is 3" by 3" (7.5 × 7.5 cm). Lay one square on top of the other. Cut the square in half into two rectangles, and stack these halves on top of each other, being sure that the colors alternate throughout.
3. Cut this stack in half and stack again. Cut once more and stack. Compress the stack somewhat to snug the sheets together, and to eliminate any air bubbles.
4. Reduce the cane to the size you need (see square cane instructions).

5. A loaf cane being assembled.

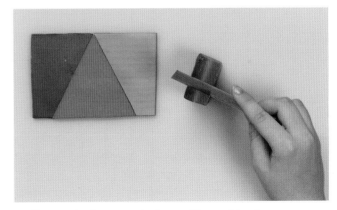

6. Slicing a loaf cane made from a Skinner blend.

7. A face cane was used in the Cartoon Bracelet project.

Cartoon Face Cane

This cane is a little more involved but not at all difficult.

1. Start by making the eyes. Use one of the bull's-eye canes for this. A black center with a white exterior works well. Wrap a second white sheet of clay around it to fatten up the white part of the eye. Add a thin sheet of black. Roll the cane to about ¾" (2 cm) in diameter, and 5" (12.5 cm) long. Cut the cane in half. You now have two eyes.

2. Choose a color for the face. It does not have to be a typical flesh tone. This is a cartoon face, so anything goes: mint green, pastel pink, robin's egg blue, sunny yellow, pale violet, you name it. Wrap a sheet of the color you choose for the face around both eye canes and set the piece aside.

3. You can add a nose to your face, or not. Make it fairly small. Two simple dots can represent it. For these, roll out a log of black that is ¼" (6 mm) in diameter and 5" (12.5 cm) long. Wrap it with a sheet of the face color. Cut in half, press the two halves against each other, and then wrap both with another sheet of the face color. You now have your nose.

4. The mouth can be a simple curved line of black, to resemble a smile. It can be a circle of color, which looks as if the character is saying "Oooooo." It can be a half-circle that looks like lips on a closed mouth. Whichever type you choose, make it 2½" (6.4 cm) in length and of a diameter in proportion to the rest of the face. A mouth can be quite large, however, so don't skimp on it. Outline the mouth with black and then wrap it with the face color.

5. Once all of your face features are made, they need to be assembled and have the spaces between them filled in with the face color. Look at the spaces and make snakelike pieces of the right shape to fit into them. Don't leave any spaces empty, as these will distort the face when the cane is being reduced.

6. Once it is all filled in, squeeze the cane gently, turning it around and around as you work to make sure that all

8. Face canes, large and small, plus a few loaf and leaf canes.

of the clay is snugged together and there are no gaps to be seen. Wrap several sheets of face color around this cane to fatten out the face.

7. Begin to reduce the cane by squeezing, pulling, and rolling. Don't do this too fast. Just take it easy and gently feel it extruding into a longer, thinner piece. When it's about half its original size, cut it in half and set one-half aside for later use. Continue reducing the remaining half, cutting pieces from it at various sizes that will fit on the project for which you will be using it (see the Chunky Cartoon Bracelet project).

9. Smooch Bowl uses a face cane. By Denita Johnson.

Flower and Leaf Canes

Make these beautiful flowers in just about any color or combination of colors your creative imagination calls for. The same goes for the leaves. My favorite leaves are ones done with a blue and white Skinner blend, rather than green, or maybe a white and deep purple Skinner blend. The ones shown here are done in the more traditional white and green, however. See Photo 10 for all steps in making the leaf and flower canes.

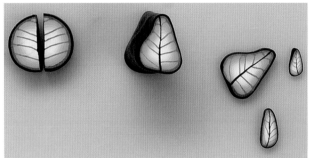

10. Making leaf and flower canes. Top, left to right: several steps in making a flower cane, and at right, the reduced cane. Left: several steps in making a leaf cane.

Flower Cane

Materials for Flower Cane

Kato polymer clay:

Purple, 4½ oz (126 g)

White, 5 oz (140 g)

Sea green, 2 oz (56 g)

Acrylic roller or brayer, or pasta machine

Sharp blade

1. Lighten 3½ oz (98 g) of the purple clay with ½ oz (14 g) of white clay to make 4 oz (112 g) of violet.

2. Condition and roll out a log of violet clay 10" (25 cm) long and ½" (1.25 cm) thick. Pinch the log into a triangle-shape snake. If you look at it from the side it is a tall triangle. Cut the triangle snake into five 2" (5 cm) lengths.

3. Condition and roll 4 oz (112 g) of the white clay into a log that is 12" (30.5 cm) long, and pinch it into a triangle-shaped snake like the violet snake. Cut the white snake into six 2" (5 cm) lengths. Set each white piece on its shortest side with a triangle point up, so the

pieces are side by side. Insert a violet triangle, with a point down, in between each pair of white triangles (see Photo 11).

4. Press the triangles together tightly at the sides, until the whole unit of 11 triangles is about 1" (2.5 cm) wide. Roll the piece into a round cane; then roll until the cane is 10" (25 cm) long. Cut the cane into five 2" (5 cm) lengths. These will become the flower petals.

5. Condition the green clay and roll it into a snake 12" (30.5 cm) long. Cut the snake into six 2" (5 cm) long pieces. Place the 5 violet-and-white cane pieces you made earlier evenly around one of the 2" long green snake pieces; the latter will become the flower center. Also insert one green snake piece between each pair of violet-and-white petal canes around the green center. Compact the piece tightly to make sure there are no gaps; this will form the flower shape. You can see a slice of this cane in Photo 11 (large cane).

6. Roll out ½ oz (14 g) of the dark purple clay on the #4 (⁵⁄₆₄"or 2 mm) setting of the pasta machine, or use a brayer to roll it to that thickness. Wrap the sheet around the compacted flower cane. Reduce the cane to the size that will work for whatever project you are doing.

Leaf Cane

A leaf cane is extremely useful for various projects. Use this one with the flower cane, or use leaves by themselves in groups of three with a few polymer clay berries near the stem area. Vary the colors to suit your needs.

Materials for Leaf Cane

Kato polymer clay:

Sea green, 2 oz (56 g)	
White, 2 oz (56 g) + a walnut-sized piece	
Purple, 3 oz (84 g)	

Very sharp blade

Pasta machine

1. See Photo 10 and the diagram for the steps in making the leaf cane. Using 2 oz (56 g) of the green and 2 oz of the white clay, make a Skinner blend (see pages 34 to 36). When you roll the blend up, you can have the lightest section on the inside or on the outside of the roll. See which you like best. In the canes shown here, the white was on the inside. Roll the entire Skinner blend tightly, and then slowly press downward, rolling it slightly to smooth the outside surface. Press down again, and continue until your cane is 3" (7.5 cm) tall or less. If the roll is any taller, it will be difficult to make the necessary cuts.

2. Set the roll on the work surface with the end up. Make 4 or 5 parallel cuts across top of the clay roll, cutting from the top down, all the way through, as shown in the diagram (11a). Leave the pieces in place for now.

3. Mix ½ oz (14 g) of the purple clay with the walnut-sized piece of white clay to make violet. Roll it into a sheet on the #5 (¹⁄₁₆" or 1.6 mm) setting of the pasta

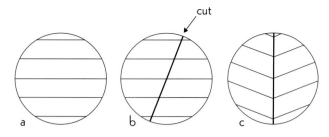

11: Three basic steps in making a leaf cane. a. Make 5 horizontal cuts. Add color in between. b. Make a diagonal cut. c. Put a dark color in between the halves, after flipping one-half over.

machine. Between each pair of cut pieces, insert a small sheet of violet clay that is close in size to the diameter of the cane. Trim the excess violet sheets to fit the shape of the cane so none extends further than the outside. Then press the cane pieces back together snugly into a cylinder shape.

4. Rotate your cane on the table so the violet lines are horizontal. Make one cut across the top of the cane going down through the cane, cutting diagonally from 1 o'clock to 7 o'clock across all the lines and dividing the cane in half (11b). Flip one-half of the cane upside down. Roll a very thin sheet of the remaining purple clay on the #5 setting of the pasta machine, and insert it between the two halves of the cane. Then snug the two halves together (11c). Trim off any excess purple clay. Wrap the cane with a #5 sheet of violet clay. Wrap it again with a #5 sheet of purple clay.

5. Reduce the cane down to the size you need for your leaves. You may want to save some of the cane at various sizes along the way. Once you have a size you want, pinch the cane into a triangle with rounded corners, like a leaf (see photo). Let the cane sit for at least an hour before slicing.

8 ANTIQUING

Antiquing is easy and fast. There are a number of ways to antique a piece, but the easiest way is to use acrylic paint. Two of the most popular antiquing colors are burnt umber and burnt sienna, but you can antique with just about any color, including white on dark pieces, red on black, and black on red.

Method 1 with Acrylic Paint

1. You need a stiff brush. Load the brush with the paint and begin dabbing it onto the surface of the baked clay, to get the paint into all the recessed areas, until you have covered the entire surface.

2. Wash your brush and put it aside. With your fingers, rub the paint around and around on the surface of the clay. When the paint starts to get a little dry, use a paper towel to rub off most of it. Wash and dry your hands.

4. Continue rubbing off the paint until you get the desired effect. At times you may want to leave more of it on the surface; at other times you may want it only in the recesses. Let dry completely.

You can also antique with acrylic metallic paints such as copper, gold, or silver. These paints dry very fast, so work quickly. The recessed areas will hold the glint of polished metal. There are also some wonderful acrylic enhancers available in either verdigris (weathered copper) or rust finish. These have tiny bits of grit in them that will build up in areas on the surface of the clay and will look much like the real thing.

Method 2 with Acrylic Paint

1. Coat the piece with paint exactly as in Method 1, but instead of wiping off the excess paint, let all of the paint dry on the surface.

1. Ivory bead being antiqued with burnt umber paint.

2. When completely dry, use sandpaper to remove all except the paint in the recesses. This method works very well for impressed translucent pieces, as you can smooth and shine the surface as you remove the paint.

Chemical Antiquing

Chemical antiquing solutions are also available, which can be used with the clay. You can achieve some wonderful effects with these solutions, including copper with a thick verdigris patina and rusty iron.

1. Since you will be working with very strong chemicals, be certain you follow the directions exactly. Work in a well-ventilated area and keep all of these solutions away from young children.

2. Paint on the metallic undercoat and, while it is still wet, go over it with a patina solution.

3. Set the piece in a window or somewhere with a good airflow. Ignore it for several hours. When you come back to it, you'll be delighted with the change.

4. The patina surface has a tendency to rub off with use. It is an actual patina, exactly the same as that formed outdoors on all copper surfaces. On jewelry or other items that will be handled a lot, give the antiqued surface a coating of matte glaze for protection.

9 CRACKLING

When the clay has the appearance of being crackled, it truly looks ancient. A number of crackling products are on the market today. Try out various products and see what works for you.

1. Most of these are two-step products. A coating of one type is applied to the clay and let dry to a certain stage.

2. A second type of coating is then applied and let dry.

3. With some, you can see the crackling with no trouble. With others, you will need to apply some acrylic paint that is darker than the surface of the piece, and then wipe off the excess. The paint will sink into the cracks and make them show.

4. Even though many of the crackling mediums say that the crackling will start immediately after applying the second solution, this doesn't always happen. If you don't see any crackling during the first half-hour or so, put the piece aside and check it the next day or several days later. You may be pleasantly surprised. If not, change your brand of crackle medium and try again.

1. Several examples of crackle technique.

10 GILDING

A variety of gilding methods are available to add highlights to the clay, some for baked and some for raw clay.

Metallic foils. Metallic foils come in the real thing or in imitation form. Real metallic foils are quite expensive, but hold up very well and do not change color over time. Imitation foils are inexpensive; these are what many people use. Any foil that is on the surface of the clay needs to be coated with a clay-compatible glaze, with liquid clay, or with some other substance in order to protect it.

Mica and Metallic Powders. Mica and metallic powders work well with the clay and come in many different colors as well as

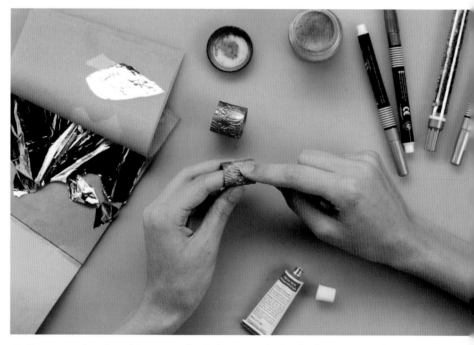

1. Some supplies for gilding: metallic foil, mica powder, leafing pens, and rub-on wax. In hands, applying gold mica powder.

gold, silver, copper, and bronze. Be sure to wear a dust mask when using these products. Metallic powders can be toxic, and it is not wise to inhale mica powders.

Powders are generally used on unbaked clay. They can be brushed on, drawn on with a clay shaper, gilded on with your fingertip, or stamped on with a rubber stamp. After baking, the powders need to be coated in order to protect them, using a clay-compatible glaze.

Metallic waxes and leafing pens: Metallic wax is a rub-on type of product, used after the clay is baked. It gives a soft, subtle metal look to the clay. It comes in many colors, including classic gold, old gold, silver, pewter, and copper. Leafing pens are also used on baked clay. They are much brighter than the metallic waxes and should probably be used sparingly. They come in gold, silver, and copper. If you sand and buff the area on which you will be using the leafing pen, the results will be much smoother and brighter. Not all leafing pens are compatible with the clay. The Krylon brand works well.

11 SANDING AND BUFFING

Sanding

Sometimes you may want a very smooth surface and a nice shine or sheen. Sanding is easy to do, as long as the piece isn't too small. Some people use just one grit of wet/dry sandpaper, while others use up to 6 different grits. The higher the number, the finer the grit. Some people believe you should never go below a 400-grit paper and others think it's necessary to go as high as 2500 grit. My belief is that you should use whatever method gets the job done to your satisfaction. If a piece is fairly smooth out of the oven, I use only a 400-grit and a 600-grit with excellent results. If it is a bit rough, I may add a 320-grit to begin with.

Wet/dry sandpaper (the kind used for automobiles) can be used wet without falling apart, an advantage in keeping clay dust out of your lungs. Sanding should not take a long time. You can only get the surface of the

baked clay so smooth. If you have a lot of pieces to sand, take a bowl of water, a towel, and sit in front of the TV and watch/listen to a good old movie, or listen to talk radio. The sanding time will fly by.

Buffing

The results of your buffing will only be as good as your sanding. A well-sanded piece can be buffed to look like glass. Some people manage to buff their work using a small Dremel™ tool equipped with a cotton or muslin wheel. Others feel that a small jewelry buffing wheel with variable speed is best. Some prefer a full-size grinder type of machine in which the grinding wheel is replaced with a soft, one-stitch cotton or muslin wheel, which has only one line of stitching around the wheel. The latter seems to be the best choice for me.

If you choose to use the Dremel tool, be very careful, as it can easily dig into the clay and make an ugly trench. You could also use a cotton cloth for buffing, which will make a nice sheen.

If you are using a bench-type wheel, there are certain things you should be aware of. The wheel can torque a piece out of your hands and fling it across the room. If this happens, just let it go. Whatever you do, don't reach over or around the machine to try and stop it. Some part of you will probably be caught in the machine if you do. Torquing happens. It's a fact of

1. Using a buffing wheel.

buffing life. Don't let it scare you. Just pick up your piece, dust it off, and go on with your work.

There are some basic rules for using all power tools and they apply here too. If you have long hair, tie it back before you start so it won't get caught in the equipment. Do not wear any jewelry that is long enough to get caught in the machinery, and no bangle bracelets. Don't wear extremely loose or baggy clothing. Never ever look away from the work you are doing on the machine. All sorts of things can happen if you do. If you want to look up at someone or something, pull the piece away from the wheel while you look. Wear eye protection such as safety goggles when buffing.

When you are buffing a piece, it should be held against the lower portion of the wheel (see photo on page 49). Remove the guard shield from your machine, if it has one, as it makes it impossible to buff at the correct area of the wheel. Do not stab at the wheel with the edge of a piece; it will probably get slammed out of your fingers and shot down against the floor. The piece should be held by one hand and supported by your other. You will learn, as you practice, just how much pressure is necessary to bring up a good shine. Too much pressure can burn and blister the clay. Too little will not raise the shine.

Once you have practiced buffing for a while, you will love doing it. You will love the look and feel of the piece as the colors become richer. It will give you a whole new perspective on working with polymer clay.

12 GLAZING AND SEALING

Glazing or sealing baked clay is often unnecessary. However, sometimes you will use a surface technique that needs a protective coating over it. Perhaps some foil or powders need protecting. If you do not have access to a buffing wheel and still want a nice shine, glazing and sealing are alternatives.

Not all the materials made for glazing or sealing are compatible with polymer clay. Some will stay sticky forever. Some will peel off. Most clear nail polishes are not compatible. Most spray-on glazes are not suited to polymer clay. Use products made especially for polymer clay, such as those made by FIMO, Sculpey, and Premo! Sculpey. Alternately, you can use Flecto Diamond Varathane Elite or Future acrylic floor finish.

Glazes can be brushed on or sprayed using a non-aerosol bottle. Some items can be dipped in glaze if

1. Jewelry glazed with clay-compatible glaze.

you are careful to avoid drips. Future floor finish is a very thin solution that can be brushed on, used as a dip, or mopped on with a piece of soft cotton T-shirt material.

13 CREATING FAUX MATERIALS

It would take another book to explain all of the techniques for transforming your clay into look-alikes of jade, ivory, bone, wood, amber, coral, jet, tortoise shell, jasper, glass, etc. Polymer clay can be manipulated to look very much like these and many other substances. To scope out the possibilities, look at the many books on beads through the ages and books on working with polymer clay. With a little experimentation, you will soon find a way to recreate the appearance of just about any material you desire. Here are instructions for a few popular impostors to start you off.

Jade

One of my favorite ways to make faux jade is with a combination of translucent clay and several shades of green embossing powders. Work the embossing powders into the clay, a small amount at a time. As a rule, the clay will be darker after baking when using this method, so be cautious with your additions of the powder.

Another nice jade effect is made with translucent clay mixed with a small amount of green opaque clay and a tiny touch of orange to desaturate the green somewhat (make it grayer). When adding any color to translucent clay, start with a very small amount of color and increase from there as necessary.

Turquoise

Start with turquoise clay or a combination of turquoise and a small amount of green, depending on the type of turquoise you are trying to imitate. Study real turquoise to discover just how many colors and types of turquoise there are, and then experiment until you are able to recreate the ones you like. Here are some recipes to get you started.

2. Examples of faux turquoise.

Rough Turquoise
1. The polymer clay should be chopped into tiny pieces or grains and then pressed together, but not so hard as to totally blend the small individual bits of clay. Using a food processor to do the chopping will result in a rounder type of grain than chopping by hand.
2. Grate a small amount of black clay and add to the turquoise before forming your piece.
3. Use a rough piece of tree bark to impress the surface of the clay to give further dimension to it.

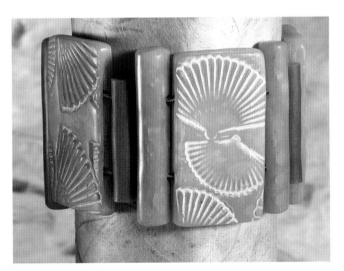

1. A faux jade bracelet.

4. Antique the piece by rubbing burnt umber acrylic paint over it, making sure you hit all the recessed areas. Wipe the surface paint off with a paper towel. While the paint is still wet, press some dark potting soil or plain earth into the clay, and brush off the excess.

5. After baking, sand the surface, and then buff by machine or by hand.

Smooth Turquoise

1. Start with translucent clay, add turquoise-colored embossing powder, and mix them together.

2. Add a light sprinkling of black embossing powder and mix in slightly. Form your piece, bake; then sand and buff.

Ivory, Bone, and Wood

Simple Ivory or Bone

Sometimes just mixing an old ivory color of clay will be enough for your project. Try: white, beige/ecru and a bit of yellow; or white and a small amount of gold; or beige/ecru and translucent. Play with the amounts until you find what works for your needs.

Striated Ivory

1. Roll out long snakes of white, beige/ecru, and translucent and then bundle them together.

2. Cut the bundles in 3 pieces and bundle again. Roll out the bundle into a long snake, cut in 3 pieces, bundle again, and roll out. Repeat this a number of times. As you do this, the diameter of each of the original snakes will become smaller. If you cut off an end piece from the bundle, you can see just how small the diameters are. If you go too far, however, the colors will blend together and you will lose the striated effect.

3. When the diameters of the snakes are as small as you want them, cut the clay into 3 or 6 pieces, depending on how wide you want the piece to be, and align them side by side, snuggling them close to each other. You can now roll them out lengthwise with a hand roller to a sheet of the thickness you need for whatever project you are doing. If you roll sideways, your striations will get wider.

3. Example of faux ivory.

Wood

You can get the look of wood by varying this technique, using slightly darker tones or wider striations.

Amber

Some ambers are very yellow, others are quite orange, and some have a lot of red in them. Combining translucent clay with small amounts of opaque orange, golden yellow, and a dark red such as Bordeaux or alizarin crimson can make a beautiful amber look-alike.

1. Mix the translucent and yellow clays in a ratio of 1:1.

2. Add only a very small amount of orange at a time, mixing well after each addition, until you get a warm tone.

3. Add just a tiny bit of the red, as it is a highly saturated color.

You will discover that you also can adjust the mixture to resemble a variety of coral tones.

14 ROLLING BEADS

Bicone beads are used in some projects in the book. For rolling a bicone bead (a bead shaped like two cones joined at the tops), the only tool you need is a lid from a wide-mouthed jar or a small square of acrylic plastic, 3" x 3" (7.5 cm x 7.5 cm). Form your clay into a ball of the size bead you want. Hold the jar lid or acrylic square horizontally over your work surface and place the ball of clay under it. Roll it for a minute and look at the results (see Photo 1). Your bead should be a well-shaped bicone.

1. Rolling a bicone bead, using a jar top as a roller. On table, a completed bicone bead.

Bead rollers are handy items to have if you are going to be making a lot of beads. With these you can roll round, oval, and bicone shapes in a variety of sizes fairly quickly. Bead rollers are available over the Internet; they can also be handmade if you are good at that type of thing.

When using a bead roller, the right amount of clay is crucial to your success. Most of the rollers come with instructions on how to measure the clay. If you make your own roller or get a set without instructions, roll out a sheet of clay on the widest setting of the pasta machine; then use a small round cutter to cut out pieces that are all the same size. Try making several sizes of circle. It takes some experimenting to find out which size cutter is needed to roll a particular size bead, and whether you need one, two or more circles. When you find this out, mark it down somewhere for reference.

2. Rolling a bead with a bead roller; on table, examples of beads made with various sizes of roller.

Once you have found the right amount of clay for a certain size of bead, hand-roll the clay into a ball and place that into the trough of the bead roller. Place the correct top on the trough and then use the handle on the top to slide the top (and ball of clay) back and forth until the bead is formed (Photo 2).

To roll a bead with more than one color of clay on the surface that you want to swirl, set the clay ball at the end of the roller that is nearest to you. Roll across to the far end, pick up the clay, move it back to the start of the roller, and place it down so it is oriented in exactly the same way as when you picked it up. Roll again. Repeat this over and over until you get the amount of swirling you want.

15 PUNCH CUTTERS

Those nifty little punches that are made to use with paper can also be used with the clay. Care must be taken when using them, however. Raw clay that is rolled into a very thin sheet and then dusted well with cornstarch can be punched very easily. The punched-out piece can then be wiped of the cornstarch and laid down onto another clay surface. If you want to punch baked clay, the sheet must be very, very thin. Warming the clay also helps. If the sheet is too thick, it may not fit into the punch or it may damage it when you try to punch. Punches come in a variety of designs.

1. Using a punch cutter.

16 INCLUSIONS

You can mix a great many things into polymer clay for a wide variety of effects without damaging the structural integrity of the clay, including embossing powders, mica powders and flakes, colored and natural sand, fibers and threads, herbs and spices, and seeds. Jump in and experiment. Keep a record of what you do so that you can repeat your successes. Be sure to wear a mask when working with powders.

Embossing Powders

Embossing powder mixed into translucent polymer clay will give the baked clay a convincing look of stone without the hard-to-deal-with fibers that are in stone-look clays. You can get many other effects besides stone. When embossing powder is added to layers of different-colored clays, they take on many other appearances. There are no standard measurements for how much powder to use with a certain amount of clay. A lot of powder will cause the clay to be quite dark; a small amount will give a paler appearance.

Embossing powders can be purchased at rubber stamp supply stores or on the Internet, and from polymer clay supply companies.

1. Use translucent or tinted translucent clay only. Roll the clay into a sheet on the #1 setting (⅛" or 3.2 mm)

of the pasta machine; then spoon or shake about one-quarter of the amount of powder you plan to use onto one-half of the clay's surface. Leave a good margin of bare clay around the edges.

2. Fold the unpowdered half of the clay over on top of the powdered clay. Start by pressing in the middle of the piece and work toward the edges. This will help to eliminate most of the trapped air. Seal the edges of bare clay tightly.

3. Run this packet of clay through the pasta machine on the #1 setting, folded end first. You will still get a few air bubbles, but these will work out as you continue to mix.

4. Fold the piece again and run it through the machine again and again, until the powder is evenly distributed throughout the clay.

5. Repeat Steps 1 through 4 with another quarter of the embossing powder; continue until you have used it all. This process makes somewhat of a mess. Some powder may spill out, so put down paper towels or something else to catch it; you can then return it to the clay and keep mixing.

Mica Powders and Flakes

To use mica powders and flakes as inclusions, experiment with the amounts to see what results you get. These also require translucent clay for the best results.

Kitchen and Garden Powders and Herbs

Colored or plain sand, seeds, herbs, and spices can be used as inclusions; this takes some experimenting. Using translucent clay, start with a level teaspoon (5 mL) of any one or more of these inclusions. Surprising results often occur when working with these inclusions. Try black pepper, paprika, red cayenne pepper, pumpkin pie spice, rosemary leaves, oregano, dill seed, and coffee. Use a variety of flower petals such as rose, lavender, and gladiolas, as well as potting soil, sand, and bird seed. Dried flowers placed underneath a very thin layer of translucent clay create a lovely effect rather like an Impressionist painting, with diffuse colors.

1. Clay with spice inclusions.

17 INKS AND PAINTS

Many products available now can be used with polymer clay to great advantage. Most acrylic paints are compatible with the clay, including beautiful metallics and inference colors, which can be used when making a mokume gane pad. Transparent inks create unusual effects. Piñata inks from Jacquard are great to experiment with and have many wonderful uses. These can be painted or stamped onto thin sheets of translucent clay backed by foil for use in various types of mokume gane.

18 BURIED TREASURE SURFACE TECHNIQUE

This delightful surface technique, invented by Jeanette Roberts, creates a dimensional surface that seems to glow from within. It can be used for a wide variety of projects.

There are two versions of this technique: one uses plastic-backed metallic foils and the other uses mica powders. The foil technique works best for fairly small surfaces. The mica powder method seems to work best for larger sheets of clay.

The Foil Technique

1. Condition the clay and roll out a sheet on the thickest setting of the pasta machine.
2. Place a piece of the plastic-backed metallic foil such as Jones Tones or Tonertex, color side up, on top of the clay; burnish the surface well with the dull edge of a sharp blade or other burnishing tool. Make sure there aren't any bubbles or creases. Let it rest for about 5 to 15 minutes; then quickly rip off the plastic backing sheet. Your clay sheet should now be covered with the foil. If there are a few small bare spots, it shouldn't spoil the final effect.
3. If this method doesn't work well, an alternative is to burnish the foil on the piece and then use a heat gun to warm the surface slightly for about 10 seconds before ripping off the backing. Be sure you keep the heat gun continually moving and at least 10" (25 cm) away from the surface, so you don't melt the foil and bake the clay.
4. If you find you have a large bare spot, burnish another piece of foil over it and repeat the process.
5. To texture the surface with a texture sheet, apply a small amount of cornstarch to the top of the foiled surface, or else spray the texture sheet with water. Use one or the other, not both. Either of these will act as a clay release.
6. Place the foiled side of the clay against the texture sheet and run both through the pasta machine on the widest setting. If you are using other colors of foil, prepare and texture clay sheets with those colors of foil on

them also. Note: You can use a deeply etched rubber stamp to texture instead of a texture sheet.

7. If your foiled clay sheet is too thin to use by itself, prepare a second sheet of clay by running it through the pasta machine on #3 setting (³⁄₃₂" or 2.4 mm). Place the textured, foiled sheet of clay on top of the second sheet of clay, making sure not to trap air bubbles, lightly pressing as you lay the top sheet down.

8. Trim the combined sheets of clay (or single sheet if it is one thickness) to the exact size you will need for your project. If you are planning to cut the clay into squares and apply them like tiles to a clay surface or other surface, use a square cutter or paper template and sharp blade for accuracy, and cut the squares you need. Use a coating of liquid clay on the surface of the object to be tiled, to help the clay to stick.

9. After you have placed the foiled, textured clay pieces onto whatever project you have chosen, bake at the correct temperature for that clay and let the piece cool.

10. Wet-sand the surface with 320- and then 400-grit wet/dry sandpaper. This will remove the foil from the top surface of the clay, but it will remain in the recessed areas. Next, wet-sand with a 600-grit sandpaper (and higher grits if you wish) until the clay is extremely smooth.

11. Buff the piece using either a buffing wheel or other buffing device until the clay is extremely shiny. If you want a higher shine, coat the piece with one or two applications of an acrylic floor finish.

1. Jeanette Roberts' book cover and bracelet are done with with buried treasure foil technique.

Mica Powder Technique

1. Plan your project and roll out a few sheets of clay on the #1 setting (⅛" or 3.2 mm) of the pasta machine. Place about ⅛th teaspoon (.6 mL) of mica powder on the surface of a clay sheet, and use your finger to spread it around and smooth it. Tap off any excess. Make several sheets, using different colors of mica powders in this way, if you wish.

2a. Using a texture sheet. If you're using a texture sheet, place the texture sheet on the mica powdered side of the clay and run the two through the pasta machine on the widest setting. Repeat for each sheet of clay you need.

2b. Using stamps. If you're using stamps instead of a texture sheet, place the micaed clay sheet onto a sheet of waxed paper and then lay it face up on a hard floor. Center a rubber stamp on top of the clay and then carefully stand on the back of the stamp. This will help to make the deepest impression possible. Make as many stamped pieces of clay as you need. Vary the mica powder color if desired. Repeat as many times as is necessary to texture the whole sheet.

3a. Using a texture sheet. Peel clay away from the texture sheet. Cut the clay sheets into equal-sized square pieces if you are using them as tiles, or shape them as needed to fit the surface you are covering.

3b. Using stamps. Remove the stamp and peel the clay from the waxed paper. The mica powder acts as a release medium, so the clay will not stick to the stamp. Cut the stamped sheets into equal-sized square pieces if you are using them as tiles, or shape as needed.

4. Apply the clay to your project and bake at the recommended temperature for that clay; let cool. Continue as you did in Step 10 of the Foil Technique, sanding and buffing. Coat the piece with an acrylic floor finish to seal in the mica powders and add an extra shine. If you do not have access to any type of buffer, be sure you sand well and then give the piece several coats of the acrylic finish.

2. Photo album cover done with buried treasure mica powder technique, using several colors of mica powder and a square cookie cutter.

Projects

FAUX JADE & TURQUOISE BRACELETS

Designer
Dotty McMillan

Segmented bracelets are the perfect choice for using various faux techniques. The clay recipes shown here are the simplest ones possible. When I have worn this bracelet, a number of people have asked me where I got my beautiful jade bracelet. Did I tell them it's not jade, it's polymer clay? Yes, but I was tempted not to. There are various ways to make a segmented bracelet. This is just one of them. It's more precise than some of the others but is not at all difficult. Later in the project we give the instructions and materials for the turquoise bracelet shown at the top of the photo.

MATERIALS FOR JADE BRACELET

Polymer clay:

      Bleached translucent Premo! Sculpey, 6 oz (168 g)

      Leaf green Premo! Sculpey, ¼ oz (7 g)

      Orange Premo! Sculpey, ¼ oz (7 g)

      Purple Premo! Sculpey, 1 oz (28 g)

Texture sheet or rubber stamp

Titanium white acrylic paint

Paintbrush

Needle tool

Sharp blade

Wet/dry sandpaper, 220 and 400 grits

Buffing wheel or clay-compatible glaze

Gold or white jewelry elastic

Two thin aluminum knitting needles, size #1, or wooden skewers at least 10" (25.4 cm) long

Acrylic roller

Pasta machine

Paper and pencil

Cyanoacrylate glue

Ruler

Instructions for Jade Bracelet

1. Draw out the diagram (page 63) on white paper according to the measurements shown. It is 2" tall in total. The center part is 1" (2.5 cm) tall. The parts above and below it are ½" (1.3 cm) tall. You will use this diagram to cut your bracelet pieces to the correct size and to place the knitting needles or skewers where they should be to shape the holes for the elastic. You will leave the needles in the clay while it is baking. The main bracelet pieces or segments will end up about 2" (5 cm) tall and 1" (2.5 cm) wide.

2. Condition the translucent clay, set aside about 2 oz (56 g) of it for later, and then add a half-pea-sized piece of the leaf green clay to the remaining translucent clay. Mix the two together until totally blended. The color should be very pale. When baked, the color will darken. As a test, you might want to take a small amount of clay and bake it before proceeding. If it is too dark, add more translucent clay. If it is too light, add a tiny bit more green clay. If it's too green, add a very tiny bit of orange clay.

3. Once you have a jade color you are happy with, divide the green clay into 3 equal balls. Using one of the balls, roll out a sheet on the #3 setting (3⁄32" or 2.4 mm) of the pasta machine. The piece should be at least 3" (7.6 cm) wide and 6" (15.2 cm) long. Texture the surface with either a texture sheet or a rubber stamp (see pages on texturing).

4. Place the textured sheet onto the diagram that you have made, and trim along the outside lines. Then cut the piece to 5" (12.7 cm) across, using the cross lines for guidance (Photo 1). In other words, make it long enough for 5 segments, but don't cut it up into segments yet. Depending on your wrist size, you may have to adjust the number or width of the segments.

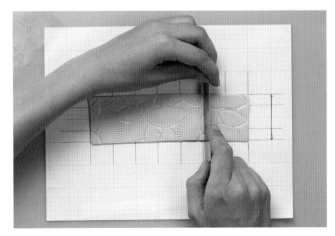

1. Cutting the textured clay to the right size.

Four segments (plus the intervening "snakes") will make a bracelet about 7½" (19 cm) long, which is an average size. The bracelets shown are this size. Remove the textured sheet of clay and set aside. Later you will want to cut one more segment than is needed so you have an extra piece in case a problem arises with one of your segments.

5. Roll out a second ball of the green clay on the #3 setting of the pasta machine. Trim this sheet to the same size as the first sheet. Lay the knitting needles on the lines shown for them on the diagram. With your fingers, press the needles into the clay (Photo 2). Roll over the needles with your acrylic roller. Press them almost all the way through the sheet of clay.

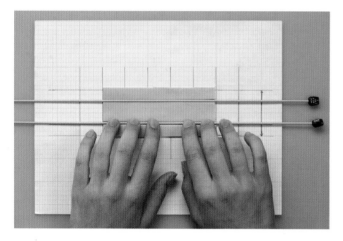

2. Pressing knitting needles into the clay for the middle layer, to make channels for the elastic.

6. Lay the first sheet on top of the second sheet, sandwiching the knitting needles or skewers between them. Be sure that the textured side is up. Carefully peel the clay and needles off the diagram paper and set aside.

Roll out the third ball of green clay on the #4 setting (⁵⁄₆₄" or 2 mm) and cut it to the same size as the other two sheets. (If you want your bracelet to be reversible, you can texture this bottom sheet also.) Fit this sheet neatly on the bottom side of the sandwiched piece. Fit the sandwiched stack on top of the diagram, with the textured side up, and use your blade to make lines in-

dicating where each segment should be cut. (Each segment should be about 1" wide, or 2.5 cm.) These are the 1" marks on your diagram.

7. Place the whole piece into the oven and bake for the required time. While the piece is still quite hot, use your blade to cut the segments apart. Don't let the piece cool first, or it will be difficult to make the cuts. If it should get cool by accident, reheat the piece for a short time and then cut.

8. Bundle any of the leftover green clay together. Add a very small amount of green to it and blend well. Roll out a snake that is approximately ¼" (0.6 cm) in diameter and at least 7" (17.8 cm) long. Place the snake on the diagram and cut it into pieces the same height as the segments, 2". Mark where the holes should be in the snakes (where the knitting needles were lined up). Remove the snakes from the diagram and finish making the holes. Bake and let cool.

9. Mix about 2 oz (56 g) of translucent clay with a large pea-size piece of purple clay. Roll this mixture into a snake that is ¼" (0.6 cm) in diameter and 6" (15.2 cm) long. Cut this piece into 2" lengths. Mark, and then make the holes in the proper places as you did for the green snake segments. Line these pieces up together and trim about ¼" off each end. This will make them shorter than the other segments, which will give your bracelet a sense of motion. Bake the green and purple snakes and let cool.

10. Sand and buff all the segments. Antique the textured side of the flat segments with titanium white acrylic paint. Wipe off any excess on the surfaces. Let dry. Rebuff them to bring the shine back. If you are using a glaze instead of buffing, sand, antique, and then glaze.

11. Cut 2 lengths of gold or white elastic jewelry cord to about 12" (30.5 cm) in length. Lay out the segments in the order shown in Photo 3. Run a length of elastic through the top holes, and another one through the bottom holes (Photo 3). Snug the ends of the elastic together and tie a square knot in each. Trim the elastic. Add a drop of cyanoacrylate or jewelry glue to each knot, and then tug on the elastic to pull each knot into a hole. There you go. Slip on your bracelet and enjoy.

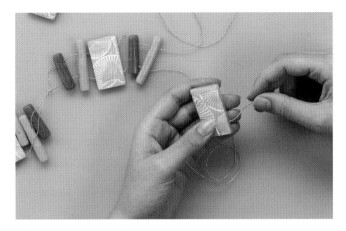

3. Stringing the bracelet sections.

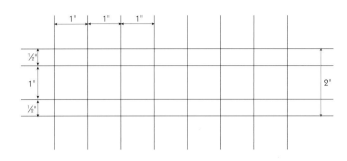

Reduced cutting diagram for bracelets. Copy or draw at 285%.

FAUX TURQUOISE BRACELET

The turquoise bracelet is made the same way as the jade bracelet, except for the color of the clay, the type of antiquing, and the shape of the spacer pieces. Make sure you measure for the size you need and change the dimensions of the segments to fit this need.

MATERIALS FOR TURQUOISE BRACELET

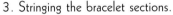

Polymer clay:

> Turquoise Premo! Sculpey, 6 oz

> Black Premo! Sculpey, 3 oz

Black jewelry elastic

Black acrylic paint

Copper leafing pen

Texture screen with small dot pattern

Texture screens with bamboo or floral pattern

Other tools as for jade bracelet

Instructions for Turquoise Bracelet

There are no colors to mix for this bracelet. Just use the turquoise and black.

1. Make the flat segments the same way as the jade segments with these exceptions: roll out the turquoise on the #3 setting (³⁄₃₂" or 2.4 mm) of the pasta machine, texture it with the bamboo texture screen, cut the textured sheet of clay to the size that will make 6 segments, and set aside. Don't cut the segments yet.

2. Roll out the black on the #3 setting. Place it on the diagram, cut the sheet of clay to the size needed for all 6 segments, and press the knitting needles into it. Cover the black clay and needles with the textured turquoise sheet of clay.

3. Roll out another sheet of turquoise on the #3 setting, texture it using a different type of texture or leave plain, and cut to the same size as the other sheets. Place the most recently made sheet on the bottom of the two sheets already assembled. Mark your cutting lines on the top layer of the clay. Note: You will need two segments cut to ½" (1.3 cm) width, in addition to the four 1" (2.5 cm) wide segments.

4. Bake, remove needles, and cut clay into segments along the lines while it is still quite warm. Cut 4 regular-width segments and cut the two extra segments ½"

(1.3 cm) wide. Turn the regular-width segments over so that the back side is up. Use your blade to bevel the top and bottom end of each segment (Photo 1). Trim ⅛" (0.3 cm) off the top and bottom end of the ½" wide pieces. Sand and buff each piece. Antique with the black acrylic paint and re-buff or glaze.

1. A textured segment with beveled edges. On the table, half-width segments.

5. Roll the black clay into a snake that is about ⅛" (0.3 cm) in diameter and 8" (20.3 cm) in length. Wrap the snake with a #5 width sheet of dragon skin textured clay (see page 39 for instructions). Make the dragon skin by layering black on top, turquoise in the middle, and black on the bottom so that when you slice off the tops of the dots, the turquoise will show through. Snug the seams of the wrapped sheet together around the snakes (Photo 2). Cut the snake into 1½" (3.8 cm) lengths. Make the holes in the proper places for the elastic (see jade bracelet for details). Bake, sand, and buff.
6. Assemble the bracelet using black elastic. Be sure to snug the knots into the holes. Add a drop of glue if necessary.

2. Making the dragon skin-covered snakes. In hand, the dragon skin wrapped snake of black clay.

7. For the turquoise bracelet pictured, I used a Krylon copper leafing pen, one of the few brands of metallic pen that is compatible with the clay. I gilded just the inside edges where the flat segments meet, to give it a slight flash of copper when it is being worn (Photo 3).

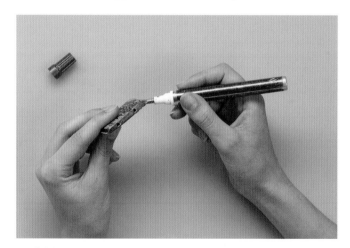

3. Gilding the edges of a bracelet section.

FAUX BRAIDED LEATHER NECKLACE

Designer
Bonnie Mray

onnie is a multitalented crafter who continually experiments with various techniques and enjoys taking them in new and different directions. Her braided necklace is the result of some of these experiments. Resembling strips of leather, this necklace is one that can be worn as well with jeans as with a cashmere sweater. Our instructions are for the dark necklace shown. I've found it can also be made using bright colors or muted pastels with beautiful results.

MATERIALS

Polymer clay:

Black Premo! Sculpey, 2½ oz (70 g) block

Gold Premo! Sculpey, two 2 oz (56 g) blocks

Pearl green Premo! Sculpey, 2 oz (56 g) block

Sharp blade

Brayer or acrylic roller

Ruler

Pasta machine

Shade-Tex® rubbing plate, leaf pattern; or other suitable texture sheet (small overall pattern)

Needle tool

Paper plate, 9" (23 cm) diameter

Cyanoacrylate glue

Wire brush

Buna-N rubber cord or other cord, about 3 mm in diameter, 20" (50.8 cm)

Spray bottle with water

1. Cut a gold block and a green block of clay in half. Mix one-half of each of these blocks to form an olive green. Condition 2 oz of black clay and the second block of gold clay. Roll each color (olive, black, and gold) into a 2½" × 9" (6.4 × 23 cm) sheet on the #3 setting (³⁄₃₂" or 2.4 mm) on the pasta machine. Stack these sheets in this order: olive green on the bottom, gold in the middle, and black on top.

2. Cut a 6" (15 cm) long piece from the stack. Set the other part aside. Roll the 6" piece through the pasta machine on the #1 setting (⅛" or 3.2 mm). Cut the stack in half lengthwise, stack, and repeat two more times (three times in all). You should now have a piece measuring about 2½" × 13" (6.4 × 33 cm).

3. Spray the texture sheet with water on the non-raised side. Place the black side of the clay against the wet side of the texture sheet. Lay the clay and texture sheet on your work surface with the clay side down and texture sheet side up. Use the brayer or an acrylic roller to roll over the texture sheet until you can see the clay come up into the design areas. Remove texture sheet from the clay and pat the clay dry with a paper towel.

4. Place the textured clay sheet on the work surface, texture side up, and use a very sharp blade to shave off thin pieces from the top of the texture until you can see the green and the gold coming through the black (Photo 1). Hold the blade in both hands, and keep it parallel to the surface. Finish shaving the entire strip.

1. Shaving off black clay to reveal colors underneath. (Actual clay strip will be 13" long.)

Trim ¼" (0.6 cm) off each side of the clay, using a ruler as your guide.

5. Start cutting ¼" (0.6 cm) wide strips into the textured clay, beginning 1½" (3.8 cm) down from one narrow end of the sheet, so they remain connected at that end. Cut 5 strips. Cut off any excess width.

6. Lay the 5 strips close together in a row, vertically. Take strip #1 (on your left) and place it over #2, under #3, over #4, and under #5. Leave #1 strip on the right. Do the same thing with strip #2 from the left. Continue working from the left to the right (Photo 2) until your shortest strip is about an inch long.

2. Braiding the necklace from left to right.

7. Lift the braided piece from the work surface and gently squeeze it together slightly. Round each end into a little round tail that is ½" (1.3 cm) in diameter and ¾" (2 cm) long. Trim the ends smooth. Use a needle tool to make a hole in each smooth end that is about ½" (1.3 cm) in depth and a little wider than your buna-N cord. Shape the braided piece into a semicircle. Place the piece on a 9" (23 cm) paper plate that is turned upside down. Place the clay where the plate slopes, which will help the piece maintain its shape. Bake for 30 minutes at the recommended temperature. Let cool.

8. Condition the leftover black clay on the #3 setting (³⁄₃₂" or 2.4 mm) of the pasta machine. Cut two 1" × 2" (2.5 × 5 cm) strips and wrap them around the round tail ends to form bell-shaped end caps. Cut to fit nicely, fold them around the tails, smooth, and form the caps. Texture the end caps with a wire brush or other tool. Use the needle tool to poke through the end caps to the holes in the braided piece. Check to make sure your cord will fit nicely into the holes.

9. Use your leftover pieces of colored clay to make two matching beads. Make a hole in each bead large enough for the cord to go through. Bake the beads along with the braided piece.

10. Cut a 20" (51 cm) length of cord, or whatever length you like as long as it will fit over your head. Thread each cord end through a bead. Place several drops of cyanoacrylate glue into the holes on the end caps of the braided piece, and insert the cord ends into the holes, being sure they are pushed in as far as possible. Hold in place for about 30 seconds. Allow glue to cure for 24 hours before wearing.

Your beautiful braided necklace is ready to show off to the world. Now, make another one in a different set of colors.

SUN CATCHER

Designer
Jeannette Faber

The secret of this colorful sun catcher is tinted Translucent Liquid Sculpey. Although the technique is remarkably simple, the results are beautiful. It's surprising how much it looks like stained glass.

MATERIALS

Polymer clay:

    Black Premo! Sculpey, 2 oz (56 g) block

    Translucent Liquid Sculpey (TLS), 2 oz (56 g) bottle

Pre-assembled glass sun catcher, 4" × 6" (10 × 15 cm) oval*

Extruder such as clay gun, and the die for medium-sized strings (if possible)

Artist's watercolor palette with cuplike spaces for mixing

Stamper's chalk or oil paints

Craft knife with a small pointed blade

Toothpicks and plastic straw

Tracing paper or photocopy of the pattern

Clear tape

Colored pencils or paint

Sun catchers can be found in some craft stores or ordered from online craft sites.

1. Clean the glass sun catcher, photocopy or trace the pattern, color it with the colors you like in pencil as a guide, and tape the edges to the back of the sun catcher. It is helpful if you use colored pencils to color the paper pattern before coloring the glass. That way you can see if you like the color combination.

2. Condition the black Sculpey and extrude it into long strings using the medium holes of the extruder tool. Or else roll a lot of very thin snakes of black clay about 1/32" (1 mm) thick. Lay a string of black extruded clay around the inner metal edge of the frame. If you don't do this, TLS will seep under the edges. You will then lose the color around the edges. Follow the pattern and lay down all the black lines in the pattern (Photo 1), which are the simulated lead canes. Use the point of the craft knife (or a toothpick) to guide the strings into place; then gently press them to the glass with your fingertips. Cut them off at the end of each line.

3. After all the lines are down, remove the sun catcher from the pattern and do a first bake at 265°F (129°C) for 15 minutes. Let the sun catcher cool completely. You now have a pattern of glass cells into which you can place the TLS.

4. Place desired amount of Liquid Sculpey into the paint cups of the palette. It is better to have too much than not enough of a color. If you run out of a color before you are finished, the chances of mixing an exact match are very slim. You can save what's left for a smaller project. Stamper's chalk works well to color the TLS because it gives intense colors and there is a lot of color variety. Use a toothpick to scrape off a little chalk into the TLS and mix thoroughly. The more chalk you use, the deeper the color will be. Use oil paints if you don't have Stamper's chalk.

5. To color the glass, cut a plastic straw in 2" (5 cm) lengths; then cut half the diameter away from the opening to make a small scoop (see Photo 2). Pour a small amount of colored TLS into the appropriate cell with the scoop. Spread it around with a toothpick, making sure to get into all the corners. TLS is self-

1. With pattern behind sun catcher, starting to make channels.

2. TLS, mixed and ready to apply.

leveling; after it settles, if the cell isn't full, add a bit more. After all the areas are colored in, rebake at 275°F for 25 minutes.

6. Now all you have to do is hang your sparkling sun catcher in a window where it will catch the sun. Morning sun is wonderful, and the bright colors of the catcher will help start the day off right. I can just picture a window filled with a variety of catchers, transmitting a rainbow of colors.

3. Finished sun catcher.

Pattern for sun catcher. Copy at 100%.

COLLECTOR'S EGG

Designer
Patricia Kimle

P atricia has been creating jewelry and fine craft items with polymer clay for over 10 years. Her work has been shown at many exhibitions. Patricia teaches clay classes around the country, as well as in Iowa, where she lives. Her collector's eggs are some of her most popular projects. Two are in the White House permanent collection. Her *Homage to William Morris Egg,* described here, was inspired by a William Morris wallpaper design.

MATERIALS

Polymer clay:

  Gold Premo! Sculpey, 2 oz (56 g)

  Black Premo! Sculpey, 2 oz (56 g)

  Burnt umber Premo! Sculpey, 2 oz (56 g)

  Extra clay (shown in red)

  Sculpey Flex clay, any color, 2 oz

  Liquid Sculpey

Chicken or goose egg shell with the contents removed

Gold acrylic paint

Mica powders for coloring decorations (e.g., green, pink, gold)

Water-based varnish

Pasta machine

Wet/dry sandpaper, 320, 400, and 600 grits

Cornstarch

Craft knife

Small paintbrush

Small containers for mixing paint

Oak tag or thin cardboard

Needle tool or sculpting tool

Small scissors

Tracing paper

White glue

Polyester batting

Small sponge (optional)

1. Mix ½ oz (14 g) each of gold, black, and burnt umber clay together until blended to a rich golden brown. Roll out the clay to ⅛" (3.2 mm) on the thickest setting on the pasta machine. Cover the eggshell with a long strip around the middle, and add two circles of the same clay on the ends (Photo 1). Blend all the seams together. Bake according to the clay package directions. Sand smooth, starting with 320-grit, then 400-grit, and ending with 600-grit sandpaper.

2. Roll out a sheet of red clay (or any color of clay you prefer) about ³⁄₁₆" (4.8 mm) thick. Trace the patterns, glue onto cardboard, and cut them out with scissors to use as templates for the flowers and leaves. With a craft knife, cut out the flower and leaf shapes from the red clay and smooth the edges so they're not ragged. Use a needle tool or sculpting tools to detail the flower and leaf veins and make dots in the center of the flower. Lay flat and bake.

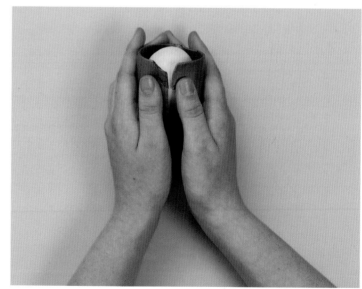

1. Wrapping the clay around the egg.

3. Making molds of leaves and flowers (Photo 2). Condition and roll the Sculpey Flex to ¼" (0.6 cm) thickness. Apply cornstarch to the surface of the Sculpey Flex clay. Press the baked leaves and flowers into the Sculpey Flex, pattern side down, until they are even with the surface of the Sculpey Flex clay. Remove the baked pieces. Bake the mold and let cool. You can see the yellow molds in Photo 2.

4. Roll a sheet of black clay ³⁄₁₆" (4.8 mm) thick. Press small amounts of the rolled clay into the flower and leaf molds, making certain to coat the mold with cornstarch before each piece is molded. Remove molded pieces and trim or smooth edges as needed with a needle tool. Apply a small amount of liquid clay to the back of each molded piece, and apply the pieces in a pleasing arrangement around the gold-covered egg.

5. Dab the gold acrylic paint over the surface of the flowers and leaves with a sponge or with the pad of your finger. Only hit the high points with the paint. Don't get paint into the recessed lines. Bake the egg in a nest of polyester batting or cotton sheeting.

6. If desired, you can make a small display cup to hold your egg, as shown on page 71. Use any remaining clay to form a small nest shape. With a needle tool, press fine lines around the edges. Highlight with gold acrylic. Bake.

7. In the small mixing cups, mix 5 or 6 colors of mica powder into the water-based varnish. Paint over the gold leaves and flowers. Let varnish dry thoroughly.

2. Stages in preparing decorations. Top, paper patterns. Original clay patterns (red clay). Left, a yellow mold. Hand is pressing clay into a mold.

Patterns for leaves and flowers. Copy at 100%.

EASEL-FRAMED PICTURES

Designer
Michelle Ross

These delightful easel-framed pictures are the result of Michelle Ross's experiments with her inkjet printer and Kato Polyclay Medium. Here she shows you not only how to do this remarkable transfer technique, but also the steps for making the fun and funky frames. Michelle is well versed in the art of demonstrating polymer clay crafts, as she has appeared many times on HGTV's "Carol Duvall Show." She has also worked in numerous other art and craft mediums.

This transfer technique differs from other transfer methods because you can use your home computer inkjet printer. Other methods require either black-and-white toner or color toner copies. It has been fairly foolproof compared with transfers made using other methods.

The image you choose can be anything you can scan into your computer or download off the Internet. It can be as personal as photos of your family or as impersonal as clip art. However, please be sure it is copyright-free. You can enhance or change colors using whatever program you have for image editing. You can also crop or resize the image to your liking.

1. Creating the transfer. If you are making many frames, print as many images as will fit on the photo paper, leaving about 1" (2.5 cm) between each image. Cut out an image, leaving a border of white paper. Paint a smooth layer of the clear Kato Polyclay medium on the image, and overlap the liquid clay onto the white areas of the paper about ⅛" to ¼" (0.3 to 0.6 cm).

MATERIALS

Polymer clay:

> Kato Clear Polyclay Liquid Medium
>
> Kato Polyclay white, 1 oz (28 g)
>
> A few other colors for the frame that coordinate with your image
>
> Cane slices that are complementary (optional)

Flat synthetic paintbrush, ¼" to ½" (0.6 to 1.3 cm) wide

Color inkjet printer and computer

Burnishing tool, such as bone folder

Epson Photo Quality inkjet matte paper #S041062

Images to transfer

Large, powerful rubber stamp heat-embossing gun (not a paint stripper)

Wire: 14 gauge (I've used copper here) and 22 gauge (or similar size)

Wire, color-coated, such as heater wire or telephone wire (optional)

Pliers: round nose, chain nose, and wire cutter

Sticks or bamboo or skewers (optional)

Scissors

Sharp tissue blade

Craft knife

Pasta machine or roller

Smooth tile or other surface on which to bake

Padded pot holder

Baking parchment or sandwich paper

Cyanoacrylate glue, gel or gap-filling type

2. The image will appear a little cloudy. Heat the coated surface with the heat-embossing gun until the image becomes shiny and clear. Use one of the larger, more powerful heat-embossing guns. When heating the clay, keep the tool moving all around, directly above the image but not so close that you cause the clay to bubble or burn. Heat for about 30 to 45 seconds per layer. Try to avoid the area of the paper that is not coated with the liquid clay. Add one or two more layers, depending on how thick you want the transfer to be, repeating the process. Let the paper cool a bit between layers.

3. Carefully peel the baked liquid clay from the paper, making sure you don't tear the thin sheet of clay (Photo 1, center). This is best achieved by loosening an edge completely across one side and then slowly peeling back the clay. Watch the two side edges to see

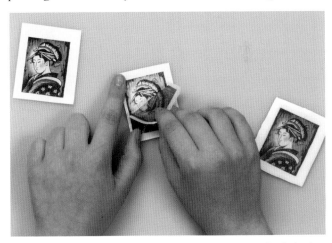

1. Left, inkjet image on paper. Middle, removing the baked liquid clay. Right, image backed by white polymer clay.

that they do not stick to the paper, causing it to tear.

4. Backing the image. Because the image is transferred onto clear clay, it will need a white clay backing. Condition and roll out a very thin sheet of white Kato Polyclay on the #5 setting (1⁄16" or 1.6 mm) of the pasta machine. Then paint a very thin coat of liquid clay onto the transfer back. Lay the white clay on a piece of baking parchment and burnish the transfer onto the white clay. Place another piece of paper on top of the transfer and burnish well, removing any air bubbles. Trim away any excess clay. Bake the transfer on the parchment for 10 to 15 minutes at the recommended temperature.

5. Removing any air bubbles. When the piece is removed from the oven, you may see some small air bubbles. If so, put it back in the oven face down on a smooth tile or glass for 10 minutes. When you remove it from the oven, use a padded pot holder (hot pad) and press on the back of the piece to push any air out. When it is just cool enough to handle, pick it up and press hard between your fingers to bond the two clay surfaces together. Trim off any excess white clay using a sharp blade so you have nice straight sides.

6. Creating the frame and easel. Your frame can be as simple or as complex as you would like it to be. Here are the steps for making the examples that are shown.

a. Use a color of your choice to create a narrow frame around the clay piece by rolling a piece of the colored clay through the pasta machine on the #3 setting (3/32" or 2.4 mm). It should be larger all around than your image. Lay and press the image into the clay and trim the clay to about 1/8" (3.2 mm) beyond the image's edges. Push the clay up around the sides of the image to form the frame. Trim if needed. This will result in a thin, colored border around the transfer.

b. Roll out another piece of clay the same color as in Step 6a on the #3 setting. Lay your framed image on top of this and trim it all around about 1" larger than the framed image. Set this aside for now.

c. Use the 14-gauge copper wire and be playful in creating two supports that will be placed on the sides next to the framed image, on top of the colored clay. You can use the colored wire, sticks, and 22-gauge wire in conjunction with the 14-gauge wire. These additions will be the two front legs of the easel. When you have the wire decoration and sticks the way you want them, place them right next to the framed image, on top of the colored clay.

d. Trim away the colored clay so that what is left are narrow (about 1/8" wide) flaps of clay, wide enough to wrap around the supports and attach to the framed image in front to hold it all together. A craft knife is helpful here to cut the clay to shape. Bend the flaps in place around the supports (see Photo 2). Add any cane pieces you wish on the frame. While creating the colored backing, use some of the backing clay to make a

2. Left, image on clay. Middle, start of the frame. Right, with the frame and one leg in place, bending the clay supports.

tube bead that will be glued to the back of the frame to support the third easel leg (see Photo 3). Bake along with the frame.

7. Glue the tube bead on the back of the baked piece about ¾" to 1" (2.5 cm) down from the top, and centered from side to side (see Photo 3). Use the 14-gauge wire to make a third leg that, when exiting one side of the tube bead, is as long as the other two legs. Leave about 2" (5 cm) of wire sticking out the other side of the tube bead. Using the round-nose pliers, make a flat coil of the 2" end. This will hold the wire in the tube, and you can bend it to any angle you wish so that the long leg will angle back and cause the completed piece to stand up on its own.

3. Back of frame, showing tube bead and third leg in place.

TINY FILIGREE BOXES

Designer
Arlene Schiek

$\mathcal{M}$ulti-toned filigree enhances these tiny boxes, which are perfect for holding rings and things or for stashing medications to carry in your purse. Boxes are not the only use for the fabulous technique, however; the filigree can be used for a wide variety of projects. You can adorn pins, pendants, candle holders, light switch plates, and beads, among many other things.

Polymer clay: 2 oz (56 g) blocks in three contrasting colors

Small commercial tins with plastic inserts

Clay gun

Embossing tool

Stamp or texture tool for patterning the bottom of the box

Typing or copy paper

Sharp blade

Craft knife

Pasta machine

1. You will need about ½ of each block to make 3 sheets of conditioned clay, each about 4" × 4" (10 × 10 cm) when rolled out on the #1 (⅛" or 3.2 mm) setting of the pasta machine. Make a Skinner blend using all 3 colors, laying them out as shown in Photo 1. (See directions for the Skinner blend on pages 34 to 36.) When fully blended, fold in half one final time and run it through the pasta machine lengthwise on the #4 (⁵⁄₆₄" or 2 mm) setting. Start at one end of the long sheet of blended clay, and slice and stack pieces that are about 2" (5 cm) wide. Compress the stacked block to make sure there is no air between the slices.

1. Skinner blend triangles and resulting block of colors.

2. Turn the block so that all 3 colors are showing on the top. Cutting from the top down, cut ½" (1.3 cm) wide, square slices off the block (Photo 1), and round them by rolling them on the work surface so they will fit into the clay gun. Load the gun and extrude at least 3 guns full of the multi-colored "threads" of clay. Use a fairly small die at the front of the gun, experimenting to find the one that makes a size of threads that will look okay on the tiny tin box.

3. Remove the plastic inserts from inside the tin box and set aside. Use some of the clay left from making the Skinner blend to make a sheet on the #5 setting

(¹⁄₁₆" or 1.6 mm) of the pasta machine. Use the sheet to cover both the top and bottom pieces of the box. Ease the clay down onto the top of the box and then over the inside edge of the tin. Use a blade or knife to trim the clay close to the edge, much like trimming a pie crust. Texture the clay for the bottom half of the box using stamps or any other texture tool you may have, and put it in place.

4. Use two lengths of the extruded clay thread, twisted together, to make a rope of clay. Place this rope around the bottom edge of the top and the top edge of the bottom piece of the box (Photo 2). Bake both pieces according to the clay manufacturer's recommendations.

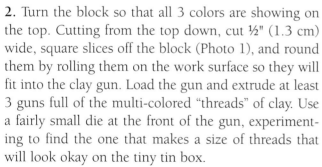

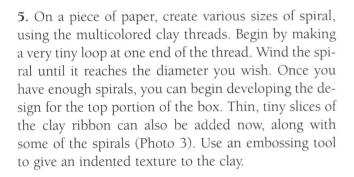

2. Bottom of a box covered with textured clay, with braid on edge.

3. Adding spirals and slices of clay threads to box top.

5. On a piece of paper, create various sizes of spiral, using the multicolored clay threads. Begin by making a very tiny loop at one end of the thread. Wind the spiral until it reaches the diameter you wish. Once you have enough spirals, you can begin developing the design for the top portion of the box. Thin, tiny slices of the clay ribbon can also be added now, along with some of the spirals (Photo 3). Use an embossing tool to give an indented texture to the clay.

6. Use your blade as a spatula to transfer the designs you've created from the paper to the box. It's a good idea to start in the center of the lid and work outward. Continue until the entire surface is covered with the filigree patterns. Bake once more. When the box is cool, put the plastic inserts back inside the box. Fit the two halves back together and your box is done. Make more boxes the same way.

DRESSING UP YOUR CLAY TOOLS

Designer
Dotty McMillan

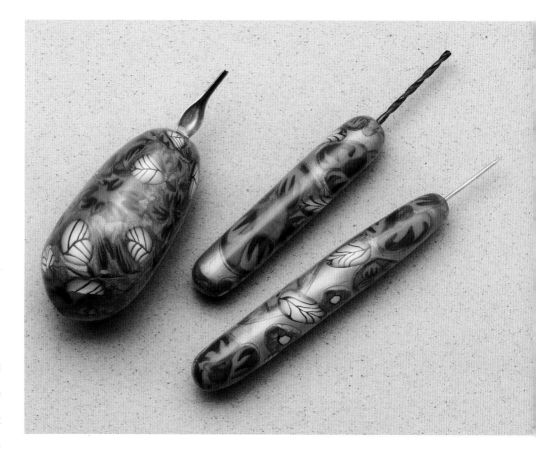

*I*n working with the clay, we all use a variety of tools. So why not dress up these basic items and make them a pleasure to look at when they are sitting on our work table? Covering the handles of these tools is easy and can be done using a wide variety of surface techniques, including mokume gane or an ethnic style with faux ivory and turquoise. Cane work can be colorful and fun, or soft and shimmery. The ones shown here were done using 3 easy canes. You can use these canes, or make others in colors you fancy. We decorated a hand drill, needle tool, and carving tool.

1. Make a leaf cane according to the instructions on page 46, but use green, white, and burnt sienna clay. You need to make two more canes for this project: a spliced flower cane and a sunburst cane. Both are made using the same blue and orange so that even though they are mixed differently for each cane, they will go together perfectly.

2. Spliced Flower Cane
a. Roll out half of the medium blue on the #1 setting (⅛" or 3.2 mm) of the pasta machine. Do the same with the orange clay. Roll the blue clay into a snake that is 12" (30.5 cm) long and about 1" (2.5 cm) in diameter. Roll the orange into a snake that is 15" (38 cm) long and 1" in diameter. Pinch each of these snakes so its profile becomes a triangle shape instead of being round. From the triangular blue clay snake, cut three 3" long (7.6 cm) pieces. From the triangular orange snake, cut four 3" long pieces. Set any excess aside.

MATERIALS

Polymer clay:

    Waste clay, 3 oz (84 g)

    Metallic gold, 4 oz (112 g)

    Pearl, 3 oz (84 g)

    Medium blue, 6 oz (168 g)

    Orange, 6 oz (168 g)

    Cadmium yellow, 1 oz (28 g)

    Dark red, 1 oz (28 g)

    Green Kato Polyclay, 3½ oz (98 g)*

    White Kato Polyclay, 3½ oz (98 g)

    Burnt Sienna Kato Polyclay, 1 oz (28 g)

    V-shaped carving bit (for hand carving)

Small drill bit in the size that you use most of the time

Purchased needle tool with metal handle

Cyanoacrylate glue

Sharp blade

Waxed paper

Wet/dry sandpaper, 400 and 600 grits

Buffing wheel or clay-compatible glaze

Pasta machine

Acrylic roller

Polyester batting

Aluminum foil (optional)

Green, white, and burnt sienna are for the leaf cane.

b. Set the 4 orange triangle pieces side by side in a row. Turn the 3 blue triangle pieces upside down and fit them in between the 3 orange pieces (see Photo 1). Snug the triangle pieces together. Roll the snugged pieces together until you get a round log. Roll the log until it is 15" (38 cm) in length. Cut the log into 5 equal pieces, each one about 3" long. Set these 5 spliced cane pieces aside.

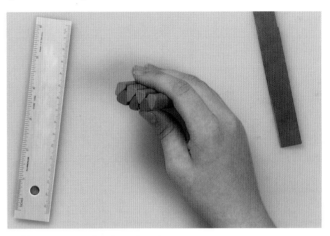

1. Starting to make the spliced cane.

c. Center of Flower Cane. Mix half of the pearl clay with ⅔ of the leftover medium blue clay. Use ⅓ of this mixture and set the other ⅔ aside. Roll the ⅓ portion into a blue pearl log that is 3" in length. The diameter of the center cane will depend on the size of the spliced blue-and-orange canes. All 5 lengths of the spliced blue-and-orange cane must fit around the diameter of the 3" long blue pearl center log (see Photo 2).

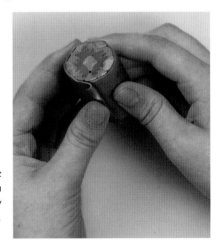

2. Side view of the spliced cane, with green + pearl clay wrapping.

d. Place the blue sides of the spliced blue-and-orange canes against the sides of the 3" blue-pearl center log, spacing them as evenly as possible around it. They should fit fairly close to one another but not overlap. Set this cane aside.

e. Mix the remaining ⅔ portion of the blue and pearl mixture with an equal portion of gold clay. This will give you a lovely soft pearl green with a slight blue overtone. Roll ⅔ of this mixture into a snake that is 15" long. Pinch into a triangle, cut into 5 pieces, and place these triangles in between the blue-and-orange canes that are around the log (Step d). Snug all the pieces together. Roll out the remaining soft pearl green clay into a thin sheet (#4 or #5 on the pasta machine) that is large enough to wrap around the flower cane (Photo 2). Roll the cane until smooth. Set aside.

3. Sunburst Cane

a. Roll the yellow clay into a log that is ¾" (1.9 cm) in diameter and 2" (5 cm) long. Wrap it with a sheet of the dark red clay that has been rolled out on the #3 setting (³⁄₃₂" or 2.4 mm) of the pasta machine. You now have a simple bull's-eye cane. Set this aside while you make the triangle snakes that will go around it.

b. For the blue triangular snakes you need to mix ⅓ pearl clay with the rest of the medium blue clay.

c. Then mix two pea-sized pieces of the blue mixture (Step 3b) into what remains of the 6 oz of orange clay. This will desaturate the orange. Also set a small amount of the blue clay aside to use for wrapping the outside of the cane.

d. Roll out the orange clay into a snake that is 18" (46 cm) long. Do the same with the blue clay. Pinch each snake so its profile becomes a triangle. Cut each into 8 pieces.

e. Place the 8 orange triangular pieces evenly around the yellow-and-red bull's-eye cane. Fit the blue triangular pieces into the spaces between the orange triangular pieces (Photo 3). Snug all the pieces together. Roll the cane until smooth. Wrap the cane with the rest of the blue clay, which has been rolled out on the #4 or #5 setting of the pasta machine.

4. Hand Drill

a. For the hand drill you need to make the entire handle and then fit it with the drill bit. Roll out a log of waste clay that is 3" (7.6 cm) long and ⅜" (1 cm) in diameter. Set aside to firm up.

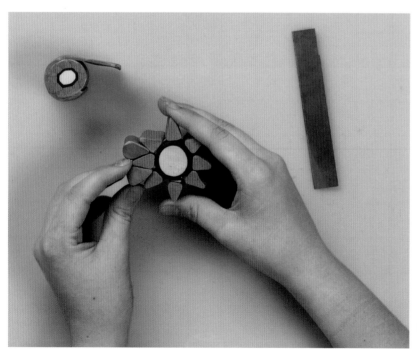

3. Assembling the sunburst cane; a finished sunburst cane, just wrapped, on table.

b. Roll a sheet of gold clay on the #1 setting of the pasta machine until it is bright and shiny. Roll it out on the #3 setting and cut a piece 3½" by 2" (8.9 × 5 cm). Place the sheet onto a piece of waxed paper.

c. Reduce the leaf cane, the spliced flower cane, and the sunburst cane to various small diameters such as ½", ¼", and ⅛" (1.3, 0.6, and 0.3 cm). Make very thin slices of each and place them randomly onto the gold sheet of clay (Photo 4). Do not overlap any at this point. Use an acrylic roller to roll these first slices smooth.

d. Cut more slices and place them onto the gold clay. Roll these smooth. Continue adding slices and rolling them in until you are pleased with the look of the surface. When you have what you want, place another piece of waxed paper over the top and roll the entire piece smooth. Remove the top piece of paper, and loosen the clay sheet from the bottom piece of wax paper. Turn it upside down so the cane-covered side is on the bottom.

e. Lay the waste clay log made in Step 4a onto one edge of the cane-covered gold clay sheet, and carefully roll the sheet around the log (Photo 5). Do not stretch it, as this can cause cracking. Overlap the sheet slightly where the edges meet and cut through both pieces to trim off excess. Remove the excess, cut-off portions of the wrapped clay, and press the edges of the wrapped clay together. Disguise the seam as much as possible.

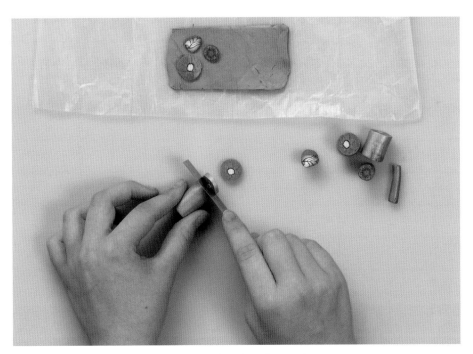

4. Starting to decorate the gold clay with reduced cane slices.

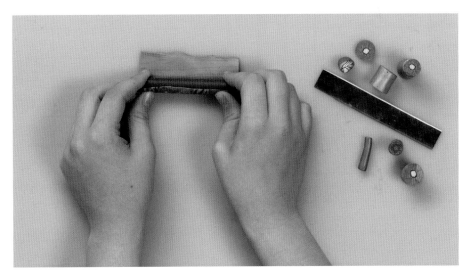

5. Wrapping the waste clay drill handle with the decorated gold clay sheet.

f. Roll the piece smooth. Trim and cover both ends of the handle with leftover pieces of the cane-covered clay. You now have a completed handle for your hand drill. Embed the smooth end of the drill bit into one end of the cane-covered handle. Bake the tool with a small amount of polyester batting underneath the drill portion so that it will not slump during the baking.

g. Let cool, sand the handle well with both grits of paper, and buff or glaze. Remove the drill bit, place some cyanoacrylate glue on the smooth end of the bit, and replace it in the hole. Let it sit for 24 hours before using to make sure it has bonded. If your drill bit should come loose, as is possible when working with extremely hard clay, just pull it out and re-glue it. You now have not only a very useful tool, but also a beautiful one.

5. Needle Tool

a. Your needle tool may come with a metal handle or a wooden one. In either case, wrap the entire handle with a sheet of waste clay that has been rolled out on the widest setting of the pasta machine. Smooth the surface well.

b. Create another decorated gold clay sheet as you did for the hand drill. You can vary the look by using slices of canes of different diameters and/or by arranging them differently.

c. Trim and smooth the clay around the back end of the tool, and bring the wrapped clay down around the needle on the other end. Snug the clay close to the needle portion, so that the clay will not be able to come off.

d. Bake; then sand and buff or glaze.

6. Carving Tool

a. To make the handle for this tool, take 2 oz (56 g) of waste clay and form a lopsided egg shape. Fit it into the palm of your hand and put your fingers forward to the narrow end. It should fit comfortably.

b. Use any scraps you may have left from the other two tools you just made, along with new cane slices, to make a decorated clay sheet for this tool. Wrap, cut, and shape this sheet over the lopsided egg (Photo 6). Smooth the surface well by rolling it between your hands and against the surface of your work table.

c. Insert the carving bit into the small end of the egg shape. Place the piece on polyester batting and bake. Let cool and then remove the carving bit. Sand and buff or glaze the handle portion. Place some cyano-acrylate glue on the smooth end of the carving bit and replace it into its hole in the handle. Wait overnight before using to make sure the glue is set.

d. If you find that cracking of the tool in the oven is a problem, you may want to use an aluminum foil core covered by a sheet of waste clay, which is then covered with the patterned clay sheet. However, small cracks will do no harm; when the piece is cool and it has been sanded and buffed, they can hardly be seen.

Now that you've made these three useful and handsome tools, think of some other tools that you can turn from ugly ducklings into lovely swans.

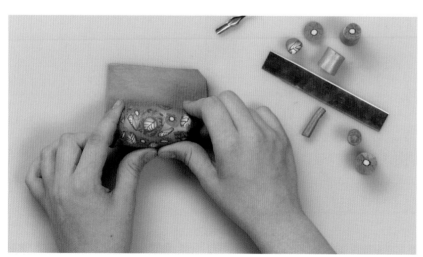

6. Wrapping a carving tool with a decorated gold clay sheet.

SQUARE PENDANT

Designer
Nancy Pollack

*I*f you like to draw and paint, or even just doodle, the image transfer technique described here allows you to wear your work as jewelry. You can scan your drawings into the computer, print them onto T-shirt transfer paper, and cut them to fit your design. The bails integrate your chain or cord into the design.

MATERIALS

Polymer clay:

Black Premo! Sculpey, 2 oz (56 g)

White Premo! Sculpey, 1 oz (28 g)

Computer

Scanner

Inkjet printer

Sheet of T-shirt transfer paper

Pasta machine

Black acrylic paint

Small, fine paintbrush

Ceramic tile that fits in oven

Copyright-free image or your own image

Cornstarch

Bone folder

Craft knife

Small square cutter (optional)

Chain or cord for stringing pendant; bead

Buna-N rubber cord, just a little larger in diameter than your stringing material, and about 12" (30 cm) long

1. The square pendant shown started as a colored pencil drawing and was scanned into the computer. It was opened in Adobe PhotoShop Elements, altered using the methods available with the software, and then printed as a large design onto T-shirt transfer paper. The picture on the pendant is a small part of the large design.

2. Choose your image, and print it onto T-shirt transfer paper with an inkjet printer. Your image will determine the diameter of your stringing material and the size of your pendant. They should all work together well as a design.

3. Roll out a sheet of white clay on the #4 setting (5⁄64" or 2 mm) on the pasta machine. Choose the part of the image you want, and cut it out of the paper. Turn the cut paper, image-side down, onto the white clay. Using

a bone folder, burnish the image onto the paper, making sure that the entire image is in contact with the paper. Cut the image area out of the white clay, leaving a small border of clay. Don't remove the transfer paper from the clay. Bake the clay under the ceramic tile for at least 15 minutes, remove from the oven, and allow the image to cool completely before removing the paper. Trim the clay with the image to size.

4. Paint the sides of image piece with black acrylic paint (Photo 1). Allow paint to dry. Roll out a sheet of black clay on the #4 setting. Place the image piece on top of the black clay, right-side up, and trim, leaving a small border of black clay showing.

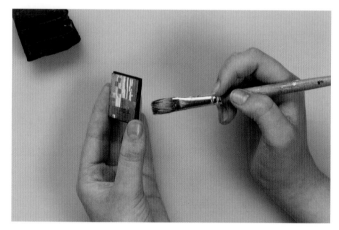

1. Paint the side of the white clay black.

5. Roll out a sheet of white clay on the #5 setting (1⁄16" or 1.6 mm). Place the image clay, with its trimmed black sheet of clay behind it, on top of the white sheet you just rolled, and trim to size, leaving a small border of white clay showing beyond the black clay.

6. Roll another sheet of black clay on the #4 setting. Place the image clay, with the black and white clay backings attached, onto this sheet (Photo 2). Trim so that there is sufficient clay on top and bottom to form the decorative rolls at the top and bottom of the pendant.

7. Roll both ends of the black clay up to the ends of the white sheet and bake for at least 15 minutes (Photo 2). Remove from the oven and cool before handling further.

8. Roll another black sheet on the #4 setting. Place the baked assembly, rotated 90°, onto the black sheet, and

trim so that there is about 2" of clay forming each side flap (Photo 3, top). You will adjust their width later. Trim the top and bottom edges of the side flaps so that they end at the top and bottom corners of the visible white sheet. They should not touch the top and bottom rolls of clay.

3. Top: the assembly placed on a new piece of black clay. Below: cutting squares out of the latest layer of black clay, which will become the chain-holders.

2. Top: black clay cut wide enough for the decorative rolls. Below: rolling up the black clay.

9. Cut 2 buna cord pieces at least 1" (2.5 cm) longer than the side bails. Lightly coat the buna cord pieces and the side flaps with cornstarch. In order to decide how much to trim the side flaps to form the side bails, lightly roll the side flaps around the buna cord, and find the point where the edge of the rolled clay will touch the edge of the baked assembly. Make a mark on the clay, unroll, and trim off the excess beyond the mark. Do this on each side. Using your square cutter or a craft knife, cut four ⁵⁄₁₆" (8 mm) square holes about ¹⁄₁₆" (1.6 mm) from the inner edge of the flaps (Photo 3, bottom).

10. Recoat the buna cord pieces with cornstarch, and roll the side flaps around them (Photo 4), making sure that the edges of the flaps are flush alongside the edges of the baked assembly. Be sure that the buna cord can move freely. Grasp the bottom end of the exposed cord, and carefully twirl it toward the inner edge of the bail. If your buna cord is curved, the curve should face in to the pendant. Without removing the buna cord from the bails, bake for at least 30 minutes.

11. Resist the temptation to remove the buna cord before the pendant is mostly cool. It should be air-

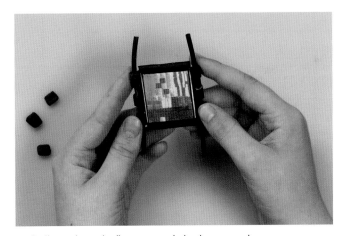

4. Roll up the side flaps around the buna cord pieces.

cooled, not cooled in cold water. To remove the buna cord, carefully twirl it again to make sure it is free, and pull it out slowly.

12. Carefully insert your stringing material down through the top of one bail, and up through the bottom of the other bail. I used a silver chain and added a bead in the center for decoration.

Now that you've done a square pendant, you may want to do a triangular one, as shown in the opener photo. Pentagons, hexagons? Your imagination is the only limit.

MERMAID PINCH PURSE

Designer
Lorie Follett

*W*hat excited me about this project is that it isn't made with the usual rock as the armature the way most of these small evening purses are made. Instead, Lorie has perfected the balloon or pinch method, which she feels is simpler. It's a delight to make; it opens up a whole new way of thinking about the clay and its uses. Once you make this one, I'm sure you will be overwhelmed with new ideas that you'd like to try using this technique.

MATERIALS

Polymer clay:

> New or leftover clay for purse in color of your choice, 2½ oz (70 g)
>
> Translucent (soft), ¼ oz (7 g)
>
> Flesh color, 1 oz (28 g)
>
> Gold, ½ oz (14 g)

Heat-resistant glitter, generous pinch

Ribbon or satin rattail cord, 1 yd (91.4 cm)

Acrylic paints

Clay-compatible glaze

Sculpting tool

Push mold for face (optional)

Paintbrushes

Drill

Polyester batting

Craft knife and scissors

Tracing paper

Pencil

1. Condition and work 2 oz (56 g) of the purse clay into a soft ball. Press your thumb into the center of the ball to create an indentation. Using a gentle pinching motion, work your way around the indentation and up the sides to form a thin-walled cup shape. If you have ever made a pinch pot with clay, this is the same method. Pinch around the piece, and then smooth the walls using your thumb and forefingers by pulling up-ward (Photo 1). Repeat. When the cup shape is as deep as it is wide, begin closing the top by pinching the clay together gently in a gathering fashion all around the upper rim until there is only enough room for one finger to fit inside the hole (Photo 2).

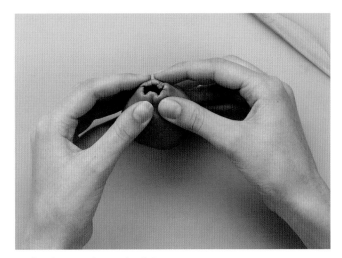

2. Pinching in the neck of the pot.

1. Making the pinch pot.

2. Gently blow into the clay to inflate the clay balloon, and pinch the opening closed, trapping the air inside. You should be able to roll the balloon of clay gently between your hands without the air escaping. For a heart-shaped purse, use the handle of a sculpting tool to create the indentation in the top and gently push the upper parts of the heart toward each other just a little. Holding the lower third of the balloon, gently pull to form the rounded point of the bottom of the heart. Once you are satisfied with the shape, bake on a bed of polyester batting according to the clay manu-facturer's directions and let cool.

3. Once the heart is cool, mix a small amount of very soft translucent clay with the heat-resistant glitter; rub this glitter mixture over the entire piece. You want this coating to cover the clay underneath (Photo 3). Once it is baked, you will be able to see through it some-what. Bake on a bed of polyester batting and let cool.

3. Rubbing on translucent clay.

4. Roll out the flesh-colored clay on the thickest setting of the pasta machine. Copy pattern onto paper and cut out the mermaid drawing for a template. You may have to resize the template somewhat to make it fit properly onto your baked heart. Place the mermaid template on top of the flesh-colored clay sheet, and use a craft knife to cut out the shape of the mermaid, including the head, torso, arm, and tail, up to where the fins start. Press the clay mermaid shape onto the heart and wrap the tail around the top right side of the heart and onto the back. Blend the edges with a sculpting tool, detailing as desired (Photo 4). Sculpt a small face and attach it onto the purse. If you prefer, use a press mold to create the face. Bake the piece once more.

5. Use a #3 setting (³⁄₃₂ or 2.4 mm) on the pasta machine to roll out a sheet of pearl clay large enough to fit the tail. Trace the tail onto the clay using the template. See Photo 5 for details of the tail. Cut the mermaid tail from the pearl clay and press onto the tail area already on the purse. Texture the tail as desired, using some mica powders if you wish. Bake again, according to the pearl clay manufacturer's directions, on a bed of polyester batting.

6. Roll out several thin snakes of gold clay for the mermaid's hair. Press one end of each snake to the top of the mermaid's head and all around the hairline. Arrange the clay strands in the direction you imagine they might flow. Press gently on the clay to adhere it to the purse. When all hair is in place, use the sculpting tool to detail by dragging the tool through the "hair" from roots to end, pushing the clay in gentle S shapes to form waves. Once you are satisfied with the hair, bake the piece again.

7. Use a craft knife to cut around the top portion of the purse to separate the bottom and top. Follow the outline of the mermaid as much as possible, being careful not to cut through the face. If the edges of the cut are rough, gently sand smooth. You can see the results of this in the finished purse in Photo 6.

8. Using the remaining purse clay or scrap clay, cut two 1" × 1" (2.5 × 2.5 cm) pieces about ⅛" (3 mm) thick. Wrap each piece around a chopstick or similar object to form a tube, and adhere the tubes to the inside of the purse on each side of the bottom part, using a small amount of liquid clay. These will hold

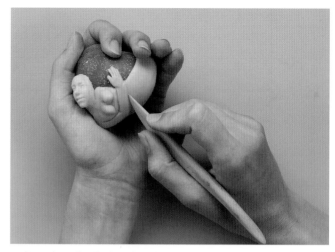

4. Detailing the flesh-colored clay

5. The back, showing the tail wrapped around.

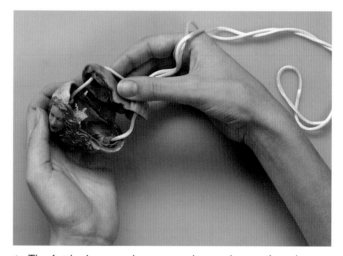

6. The finished purse, showing cut line and part of inside.

the cord for the purse. Leave room below each for the cord ends to come out and be knotted together. Remove the chopsticks. Bake.

9. Paint the details on the mermaid's eyes, lips, and eyebrows using acrylic paint. Apply a protective coat of clay-compatible glaze and allow to dry. Drill two holes in the top of the lid. Thread each end of the cord through the top of the purse, down through the clay tube inside, and tie knots at the end of each one so that it will not slip out of the tube.

You now have an adorable little evening purse or amulet to carry a bit of money, a tissue, and other small items you may need. This same technique can be used to make other small shapes: tall, narrow ones, round ones, etc. You do not have to stick to making hearts.

Pattern for mermaid. Copy at 100%.

EARRING HOLDER

Designer
Dotty McMillan

This earring holder will add a touch of charm to your dresser. The directions give dimensions for a fairly small holder. If you have a more extensive collection of earrings, or if many of them are quite long and dangly, you may wish to increase the dimensions of the holder.

ARTFUL WAYS WITH POLYMER CLAY

MATERIALS

Polymer clay:

Black, 6 to 7 oz (168 to 190 g)

Burgundy or alizarin crimson, 3 oz (84 g)

Metallic gold, 1 oz (28 g)

Liquid clay

Two brass tubes, ¼" (0.6 cm) diameter, 3½" (9 cm) long

Wooden block, ¾" thick × 6" × 3" (1.9 × 15.2 × 7.6 cm)

Ruler

Craft knife or clay knife

Paper or cardboard

White glue such as Sobo

Black acrylic paint

Texture sheets, rubber stamps, or coarse sandpaper

Cyanoacrylate glue

Small drill bit

Clay-compatible glaze such as FIMO mineral-based glaze

1. Covering the wooden block with the clay sheet.

1. Bake the wooden block at 250° F (121° C) for 10 minutes. This will rid the clay of any chemicals that are released when it is heated. Let cool. Cover all sides of the wood with white glue. Let glue dry until clear.

2. Make a pattern on paper or cardboard according to the diagram (page 94), and cut it out. Lay the wooden block onto the pattern to make sure it fits correctly. Roll out a sheet of black clay that is about 7" (17.8 cm) long and 5" (12.7 cm) wide. Texture the entire surface of the clay. Lay the pattern down on top of the textured sheet of clay and cut around it with a clay knife or other tool so your clay looks like the pattern. Place the cut-out sheet of clay on top of the wooden block; fold clay down around the sides (Photo 1). Trim any excess that extends below the bottom of the block. Snug the corners together.

3. Make two small pads of black clay that are about 1¼" (3.2 cm) square. Place one pad at each narrow end of the clay-covered wooden block (see Photo 3). Set aside while you make the upright poles.

4. Roll out the burgundy or the alizarin crimson clay on the thickest setting of the pasta machine. Texture the surface with a small, all-over pattern using a texture sheet or rubber stamp, or else use some very rough sandpaper to texture. Divide the sheet of clay in half, and wrap one sheet around each of the brass tubes, leaving 1" (2.5 cm) of bare brass on one end (Photo 2). Cut the clay to fit the tube, and smooth and disguise the seam. Slowly and carefully press the bare end of the tube into the square pad of black clay (Photo 3). Make sure that the red clay on the tubes touches the black and that no brass shows. Make sure the tubes are standing straight. Snug the black pad of clay against the tube.

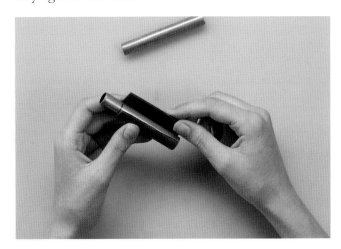

2. Wrapping clay around a brass tube.

3. Pressing the bare end of a tube into the clay block.

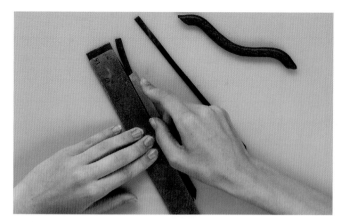

4. Cutting thin strips to hold earrings.

5. Roll out a small ball of black clay and flatten it somewhat to create a disk shape that is about 1" in diameter. Press the disk firmly on top of a clay-covered tube, making sure the black is touching the red clay on the tube. Roll out a small ball of gold clay of slightly smaller diameter and press it firmly on top of the black disk. Add a smaller black disk on top of the gold ball. Add the same parts to the second clay-covered tube. Bake the entire piece and let cool.

6. Roll a sheet of black clay on the #3 setting (3/32" or 2.4 mm). Use a fettuccini cutter, a blade, or a craft knife to cut strips (Photo 4) that are 12" to 18" (30.5 to 45.7 cm) long and 1/8" (0.3 cm) wide. Decide where you want to put the strips. If you use small earrings that do not dangle, you can put the strips close together with not much depth between them. If you have all dangle earrings, start by putting the first strip above the tubes, under the gold balls, and then space several more lower down on the tubes so that there is

room for the dangles. If you have both dangle and non-dangle earrings, space the strips accordingly. Wrap the strips around the tubes and trim off the excess. A dab of liquid clay often helps these strips to adhere to the tubes. Bake the piece again.

7. From the burgundy clay, form a yoke-shaped piece that will fit across the top of the holder and rest on the small black disks (see Photo 4). Texture the front and back of this piece. (I used a button for this.) Before baking, make sure the piece will fit nicely on top of the two tubular pieces. Bake. Use cyanoacrylate glue to attach the yoke piece to the small black disks on the tubes.

8. Use the small drill to drill holes in the black strips where you wish to place the earrings, or cut small notches on the top edge of each strip.

9. Cover everything but the wood and clay base with a clay-compatible glaze. Two (or more) coats gives an attractive finish.

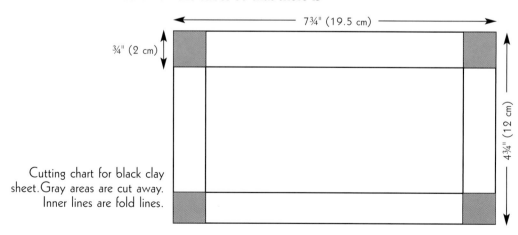

7¾" (19.5 cm)

¾" (2 cm)

4¾" (12 cm)

Cutting chart for black clay sheet. Gray areas are cut away. Inner lines are fold lines.

ARTFUL WAYS WITH POLYMER CLAY

BURIED TREASURE PHOTO BOOK

Designer
Jeanette Roberts

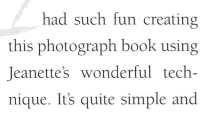 had such fun creating this photograph book using Jeanette's wonderful technique. It's quite simple and doesn't take much time. I love the multi-dimensional effect it creates. What better way to decorate a book that will hold photos of your loved ones and keep your many memories at close hand?

MATERIALS

Polymer clay:

 Black, 4 oz (112 g)

 Metallic gold, 1 oz (28 g); optional

Purchased photo book, spiral bound, with cardboard cover

Plastic-backed foil: silver, gold, and copper, or mica powders in the same colors

Sharp blade

1½" (3.8 cm) or 1" (2.5 cm) square cutter (optional)

Wet/dry sandpaper, 320, 400, and 600 grits (and finer if you wish)

White glue

Needle tool

Pasta machine

1. Remove the coil from the photo book by twisting it, and set it aside along with all but the front cover of the book. Coat the cover of the book with white glue and let dry (Photo 1).
2. Roll out a few sheets of black clay on the #1 setting (⅛" or 3.2 mm) of the pasta machine.
3. Follow the directions on the buried treasure technique for using either the plastic-backed foil or the mica powders (see page 55) for coating the surface clay. It is easiest to make a large foil- or mica-covered and textured sheet and then cut out your squares. In our case, we used mica powders (Photo 2), rubbing mica onto the surface of the clay and then running the clay through the pasta machine on the widest setting, with the texture sheet facing the mica'd side. Make 1 sheet of textured gold, 1 of textured copper, and 1 of textured silver. Use the square cutter or the blade to cut out 1½" (3.8 cm) or 1" (2.5 cm) squares from the textured and colored black clay (Photo 3).

Note: If you are using the plastic-backed foils instead of the mica powders, lay the foils, color side up, onto the sheets of clay, and then burnish the top surface with the dull edge of a blade. Burnish over the foils several times to be sure they have adhered well to the clay. Take hold of the edge of the plastic-backed foil and quickly rip the backing off. This should leave the foil on the surface of the clay. If there are areas where the foil did not adhere, just lay another piece of foil there and repeat the sequence above.

1. Paint white glue on the front cover and let it dry.

2. Rub mica powder on a sheet of clay with a finger.

3. A group of mica-covered squares, ready to be arranged.

4. Lay out the squares, alternating the colors, on the front of the photo book so that they fit evenly. Trim end pieces to fit if necessary. Press the edges of the squares carefully against the cover, but try not to flatten the textures.

5. Use a needle tool to pierce the clay where the holes for the spiral are.

6. If you wish, use a black-and-white transfer to write the word PHOTOGRAPHS onto a 1" × 4" (2.5 × 10.2 cm) strip of gold clay, rolled out on the #3 setting (3/32" or 2.4 mm) of the pasta machine. (See the section of the book on black-and-white transfers, page 25.) Don't forget to flip the word in the computer before printing and transferring it. Place the gold transfer piece in the center of the cover. Bake the cover and let cool.

7. Sand the surface of the cover, using all 3 grits of wet/dry sandpaper, from coarse to fine. Use wet sandpaper, but be very careful not to get the back cardboard side of the cover wet. As you sand, you will see the black clay become visible on the top clay surface, while the metallic foil or mica powder remains in the recesses of the design. Buff the black clay surface to a high shine.

8. Place the cover of the book on top of the photo pages, add the back cover, and twist the coil back through all of them. Your beautifully decorated Buried Treasure Photo Book is finished and ready for you to fill it with your many memories.

Photographs

PHOTOGRAPHS

Photographs

PHOTOGRAPHS

MINI-KALEIDOSCOPE TO WEAR

Designer
Dotty McMillan

Learn how to make a pendant that looks like an exquisite antique amulet. Lift it to the light and see how your pendant fragments the world around you into incredibly beautiful images. Attach a cord so that your little scope can hang around with you wherever you go. These teleidoscopes, or world scopes, are the perfect weekend project. This particular little scope uses a graphic transfer, molds, and texture sheets. However, you can substitute any type of design you wish, as long as it is scaled to fit the diminutive size of the project.

MATERIALS

Polymer clay:

> Black, 2½ oz (70 g)

> Translucent, 1 oz (28 g)

> White, 1 oz (28 g) for transfer backing

> Liquid Translucent Sculpey or Kato Polyclay Medium

Small decorative molds of flowers, borders, textures, etc.

Graphic, photo, or other transfer image, about 2" × 1¼" (5 × 3 cm)*

Colored pencils

Petit four cutter, pointed oval (preferred) or regular oval (rectangle and square will also work)

Round cutter ¾" (2 cm) in diameter

Pasta machine

Gold foil

Texture sheets of your choice

Cornstarch

Small spray bottle of water for texture sheet

Armorall

Mica powders of your choice. Super Bronze or Super Copper work well

Cyanoacrylate glue

Knitting needle about ⅛" (3 mm) diameter

Small palette knife (such as painters use)

Wet/dry sandpaper, 400 and 600 grits

Buna-N rubber cord, 1 mm thick, or other cord

Mini-kaleidoscope insert (see instructions on page 102)

Dowel, ⅝" (1.5 cm) diameter × 4" (10 cm) or more

Steel wool, size 0000 (optional)

See the transfer part of the book for instructions on how to do a black-and-white transfer that is colored with colored pencils.

1. To form the kaleidoscope case, roll out a sheet of black clay on the #2 setting (⁷⁄₆₄" or 2.8 mm) of the pasta machine. Choose a texture sheet, spray it well with water, and run it along with the black sheet of clay through the pasta machine on the #2 setting. Peel off the texture sheet and lay the black clay down on your work surface. If you do not want a textured base surface, then consider mokume gane, canework, or just a plain colored smooth surface. Cut a rectangle that is 3" (7.5 cm) tall and wide enough to wrap around the petit four cutter with just a little overlap. Wrap the clay, textured side out, around the petit four cutter and trim the ends to fit so that they butt together on what will be the back side of the kaleidoscope case (Photo 1). Smooth the join. The clay will be wider than the cutter, so be careful that you do not bend or stretch this area out of shape. Make certain that the overlap is on only one side of the cutter so that when the piece is set down to bake, there isn't any overlap there to bend.

1. Wrapping clay around an oval petit four cutter.

2. Choose the type of molded decorative pieces you wish to cover the seam on the back of the case. Make these pieces using some of the black clay. When molding a piece, use the smallest amount of clay needed to get a good impression. This helps to keep the weight of the scope to a minimum.

3. Transfer your photo or other image onto a very thin sheet of translucent clay (Photo 2), referring to the black-and-white transfer with colored pencil part of the book, page tk. Make sure that the size of the transfer will fit onto the front surface of your kaleidoscope case when baked. Add a very small amount of liquid clay to the side of the transfer piece that has the ink and colored pencil on it, and then add the gold foil. The liquid clay will help the foil adhere. Then place the transfer onto white clay, using a small amount of liquid clay to help the two to bond.

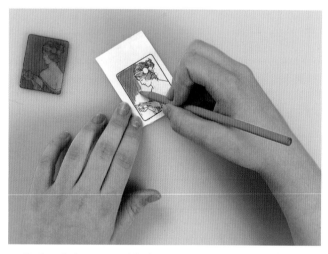

2. Right: Coloring in a black-and-white transfer. Left: Transfer on very thin sheet of translucent clay.

4. Press the transfer piece on its white clay base gently onto the front surface of your scope case. Arrange any molded or sculpted pieces you wish to add around the edges of the transfer piece. With small amounts of mica powders, lightly gild the top surfaces of the added molded pieces.

5. Bake the piece. After baking, while it is still warm, gently insert a small palette knife between the metal petit four cutter and the clay, and work it around both the top and the bottom of the case, much like loosen-ing the sides of a cake from a metal pan. If the piece is stubborn about coming off the cutter, spray a small amount of Armorall or other lubricant on the palette knife and repeat the loosening process. Slip the case off the cutter and let it finish cooling.

6. Making the inside, top, and bottom of the case. In order to hold the metal kaleidoscope insert (which you will make soon) firmly inside the case, you need to form a tube of clay. Using a sheet of black clay that is rolled out on the #2 setting (⁷⁄₆₄" or 2.8 mm) of the pasta machine, cut a piece that is 2¾" (7 cm) tall and long enough to wrap around the scope insert. Use a piece of ⅝" dowel to wrap the clay around to form the tube. The metal scope insert should fit smoothly inside this diameter. Powder the clay and the dowel with cornstarch so the clay will not stick to the dowel. It should not be wrapped too tightly or too loosely. The top end of the scope case will have a hole slightly smaller than the tube insert, which should act as a stop so that the scope insert doesn't slide all the way through. Butt the seam edges of the clay together and remove the clay tube from the dowel. Set the clay tube piece aside.

7. To form the oval top and bottom pieces of the scope case, texture a small sheet of black clay and cut out two ovals the size and shape of the case openings. Make an oval pattern from cardboard if needed. Cut a hole in the center of each piece using the ¾" circle cutter (Photo 3). Put a small amount of liquid clay around the bottom edge of the case and fit one of the oval clay pieces onto this edge. Smooth or trim the edges. Place

3. End view of scope case with oval end piece.

4. Finished scope, showing closeup of cord holders and top. On skewer, an extra holder piece of clay.

tube on the knitting needle and use it to press the tube very firmly against the liquid clay on the side of the clay kaleidoscope case. Remove the knitting needle carefully. Repeat for the second tube. Bake and let your scope case cool (Photo 4).

9. To finish, sand the areas of the scope case that have no mica powder on them, for a nice smooth-feeling piece. Buff if you wish a shine. Use 0000 steel wool for a satin matte finish. If your transfer does not sand off, you know that you placed the correct side of your translucent transfer down. If you have used mica powders anywhere on the case, coat these areas with a clay-compatible glaze.

To wear your scope, cut a piece of buna-N or other cord that is the right length to hang around your neck. Add a few inches or centimeters so that you will have enough to tie a knot at each end. Put one end of the cord through each of the cord holders. Pull the cord through and tie a knot at each end. Place a small amount of cyanoacrylate glue on the top side of each knot and then snug the cord up so that the knots are pressed against the bottom of the cord holder. Hold them in place until the glue sets. Trim off any excess cord.

this piece onto whatever surface you will be baking it on so that you do not have to lift it again. Take the clay tube that you made earlier and put a small amount of liquid clay along the bottom edges. Set the clay tube inside the clay case so that it is centered over the hole in the bottom of the case. Then put a small amount of liquid clay around the top edge of the case. Fit the second oval piece of clay on the top edge of the case. Smooth and trim. Note: If you are unable to find the Liquid Sculpey or Kato Medium, use a small amount of cyanoacrylate glue in its place.

8. If you wish to wear your mini-kaleidoscope, make pieces that will hold the cord. To form the cord holders, use the leftover circles of black clay you cut from the oval end pieces. Use the knitting needle or skewer to roll each into a tube shape. Place some liquid clay on each side at the top of the case to adhere it. Keep the

5. Front view of finished kaleidoscope.

11. See the next pages (Tiny Kaleidoscope Insert) and make an insert. Then carefully slip the kaleidoscope insert into the case, with the acrylic ball on the bottom. If it fits snugly, you do not need to do anything else. If it is somewhat loose and might slip out when the scope is turned upside down, remove it; put a small amount of the cyanoacrylate glue inside the tube near the bottom and then slip the insert back in. This will hold it firmly. Your mini-kaleidoscope is now ready to wear and to use. (Photo 5). Enjoy!

TINY KALEIDOSCOPE INSERTS

Designer
Al McMillan

These tiny inserts are not difficult to make, but they do require specific materials and measurements so that the image is good. They are for teleidoscopes (world scopes). They let you look at the world around you in beautiful fractured patterns. This insert will fit perfectly into your polymer clay kaleidoscope case.

MATERIALS

Small sheet of front surface mirror, cut into 3 pieces that are 0.430" (10.922 mm) plus or minus 0.010" (0.254 mm) wide × 2.325" (59.055 mm) plus or minus 0.020" (0.508 mm) long

Transparent acrylic ball (looks like a clear marble), ⅝" (15.875 mm)

Copper tube, 0.625" (15.875 mm) diameter × 0.014" (0.356 mm) wall × 2.625" long (66.675 mm)

Counter-bored lamp check ring (available from lamp repair shops), ⅝" (15.875) in diameter; outer diameter looks like ¾" (19.05 mm)

Glass cutter

Plastic lens, ½" (1.3 cm) diameter (2.625" or 66.675 mm focal length)

Gap-filling cyanoacrylate glue

Masking tape, 2" (5 cm) wide

Black permanent marking pen, broad point

Craft knife

1. If you are cutting your own mirrors, use a glass cutter to cut 3 pieces of the mirror, each measuring 0.430" plus or minus 0.010" wide × 2.325" plus or minus 0.020" long. Be careful not to damage the blue film that is on the glass or chip the edge of the mirror. Do not remove the blue film yet.

2. Use a strip of masking tape to attach a ruler or other straight edge to your work surface as shown in Photo 1. Tape a piece of masking tape that is 4" (10 cm) long to the table as shown in the photo. Place the 3 mirror pieces on the sticky tape as shown, with a space between each piece that is the same thickness as the mirror. Make certain that one short end of each mirror is lined up against the ruler (Photo 1). Carefully remove the blue film from each piece of mirror. Do not touch the surface of the mirrors or your final image will be marred.

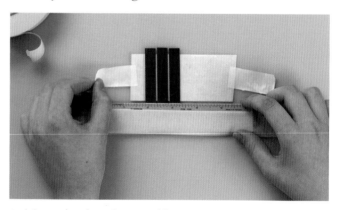

1. Mirrors lined up for assembly on tape, with ruler below.

3. Use a sharp craft blade to cut away the sticky tape along the side of the mirror on the left. Do not touch your blade against the mirror surface. Cut the tape that extends beyond the rightmost mirror to about 2" (5 cm) or more. This will free your tape and the 3 mirrors from the table. Carefully fold the 3 mirror pieces together, forming a prism whose side is an equilateral triangle (edge to surface as shown in Photo 2). Be extremely careful as you fold the 3 pieces together that

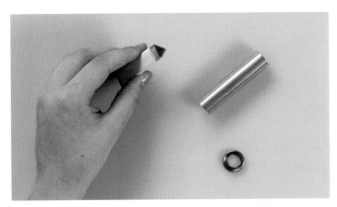

2. Assembled mirrors; check ring and tube on table.

you do not crunch the edges and damage the mirror surfaces. Wrap the 2" (5 cm) end of the tape around the outside surface of the 3 mirrors to hold them together (Photo 2). Set this assembly aside and cover to avoid getting dust or other debris inside.

4. Use your craft knife to bevel the inside edge of the brass tube to produce a flat surface about 0.020" at a 45-degree angle. Later you will need this flat surface for gluing your acrylic ball to the brass tube.

5. Lay the ⅝" (15.875 mm) brass check ring on your work surface, flat side down. Drop about 5 small drops of cyanoacrylate glue along the corridor of the inside ring (away from the opening). Insert the end of the brass tube (not the one where you beveled the inside edge) into the check ring against the glue, and hold firmly in place for 30 to 60 seconds. Put the tube and check ring aside to let the glue set up.

6. When glue is set well, insert the mirror assemblage into the brass tube. It must fit snugly to tightly. It must not be loose. Add or remove tape to provide a good snug fit. Take a look through the scope to see if there are any imperfections visible on the mirrors. Remove the mirrors from the tube. You can blow the inside clean using a compressed gas duster. Apply a coating of black permanent marker ink to one end of the mirror assembly along the outside end edges. Be extremely careful that you do not get the ink on the inside surfaces of the mirrors. You may have to go over the edge surfaces more than once. Let the ink dry thoroughly.

7. Place the brass tube on the work surface with the check ring side sitting on the work surface. Pick up a plastic lens, making certain that it is clean, and carefully drop it into the brass tube so it lies flat and is centered against the check ring. Insert the mirror assembly with the black inked ends toward the lens (Photo 3). Firmly press it in until it is at the bottom of the tube, against the lens and check ring. The mirrors must fit snugly.

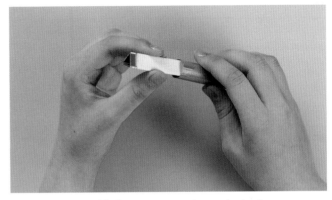

3. Inserting assembled mirrors into tube with check ring.

8. Clean the acrylic ball and set on the work surface. Run very small drops of the cyanoacrylate glue along the inside of the brass tube on the beveled end. Place this glued surface over the acrylic ball and hold in place for 30 to 60 seconds. Let the glue set up. Your mini-kaleidoscope insert is finished and ready to use with your polymer clay scope case (Photo 4).

4. Finished scope insert, showing acrylic ball and check ring.

CHUNKY CARTOON BRACELET

Designer
Dotty McMillan

This chunky segmented bracelet is one that usually brings a smile and a chuckle when people stop to look at it. Cartoon-like characters parade across the surface, surrounded by pots of flowers, sunshine, and even some clouds. It can be made with odds and ends of canes or with newly made canes that are a cinch to create. If you don't have leftover canes from other projects, just dive in and make a few of the easy ones (see Creating Canes section of book).

MATERIALS

Polymer clay:

>   Cadmium red Premo! Sculpey, 3 oz (84 g)
>
>   Black Premo! Sculpey, 2 oz (56 g)
>
>   Polymer clay canes rolled down quite small (not wider than ¾" or 2 cm): flowers, jelly rolls, checkerboards, cartoon faces, bull's-eye canes, and anything else you can make or might have on hand (vary sizes)

Ruler

Sharp blade

Knitting needle

Pasta machine and acrylic roller

Wax paper

Wooden dowel, 1½" (3.8 cm) diameter × 10" (25 cm)

Buna-N cord or other stretchable cord, 2' (61 cm)

Cornstarch

Needle tool

Wet/dry sandpaper, 320, 400, and 600 grits

Buffing wheel or clay-compatible glaze

1. Find or make a variety of simple canes. You will need 6 to 8. If you do not have a face cane, you can make one fairly easily (see page 41). The face canes can be any color that suits your fancy. Make the face canes as well as some other simple ones. Roll each down to a fairly small size, not wider than ¾" (2 cm) across, before beginning construction on the basic parts of the segmented bracelet (Photo 1). Set them aside.

1. A variety of reduced canes, including face canes.

2. Making the segments. A bracelet is made of 5 decorated segments that are strung together on stretchable cord. Instead of making each bracelet segment individually, it's faster and easier to make them all in one piece and then cut them apart just before baking, or just after baking, while they are still very warm. Use the #3 setting (³⁄₃₂" or 2.4 mm) on the pasta machine to roll the red clay. Cut out two sheets of red clay that are 7½" × 2½" (19 × 6.4 cm). (This will fit a small wrist. Increase the length of this piece for medium to large wrists, but keep the sheets the same width of 2½".) If you have any extra red clay, you can use it to make small pins to go with your bracelet.
3. Roll a sheet of black clay on the #2 setting (⁷⁄₆₄" or 2.8 mm) of the pasta machine and trim to the same size as the red sheets. From the sheet of black clay, cut two strips ½" × 7½" (1.3 × 19 cm or the same length as the red clay) and one strip 1" × 7½" (2.5 × 19 cm or the same length as the red clay). Place the black clay pieces on one of the sheets of red clay, with the 1"

black strip in the center, leaving a space for the elastics, as shown in Photo 2. In the photo you can see how the middle layer has two troughs that run from one end to the other (where the red clay shows through). This is where your buna-N cord or jewelry elastic will go later on to hold the segments together.

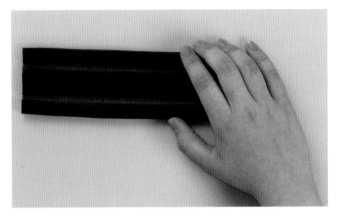

2. The bottom red layer of clay is seen below the 3 strips of black clay of the bracelet's middle layer.

4. Start your cartoon picture. Place the second sheet of cadmium red clay on your work surface and begin to build your cartoon across it, using thin cane slices (Photo 3). Keep in mind that you will be dividing the whole length of the bracelet into 5 sections later on. Lay down thin cane face slices here and there and use thin jelly roll cane slices, rolled down very small, to surround the face for hair. When laying out your figures, try to keep the main part of each face in the center of

3. Cartooning with clay on the top layer of the bracelet.

what will be one of these segments. Don't worry about arms, hands, flowerpots, clouds, etc. yet. When the heads and hair are in place, make thin slices of various canes for the clothing and add these. For arms and legs, roll out thin snakes of the face color and place them in various positions. For a hand, flatten one end of the snake and mark lines for the fingers. Cartoon figures traditionally have 3 fingers and a thumb.

5. Extras. Little flower pots can be added between the figures. A small bull's-eye cane made from white clay and wrapped with a soft gray makes nice clouds. Cut a thin slice and then distort it to form a variety of cloud shapes. Place these toward the top of the "picture," in between the figures.

6. Place your cartooned red clay sheet between two pieces of wax paper. Roll over it with an acrylic roller or other roller. Turn it over and roll the bottom side. When it feels nice and smooth, remove the wax paper. Measure the clay sheet, and trim it back to its original 7½" by 2½" (19 × 6.4 cm) size, or whatever size it was. Lay this piece on top of the other two layers of clay you have already assembled (Step 2). The black clay pieces should be in the middle. You now have a sandwich of 3 layers of clay. Looking from the side view, you can see the middle layer with its two troughs that run from one end to the other.

7. Marking the segments. Measure the distance across the piece and divide that distance by 5 to get the width of one section. Adjust your measurements to fit your own wrist. For example, if the bracelet is 7½" (19 cm) across, the width of one segment is 1½" (3.8 cm). Use a needle tool to mark the places where the bracelet segments will be cut. Decide if you want to cut before or after baking. Cutting after baking helps keep the cord holes open. If you cut before baking, use the knitting needle to make sure that the holes in the cut ends are fully open.

8. Baking and baking surface. To give your bracelet segments a slightly rounded shape so they fit your wrist better, use a 1½" diameter (3.5 cm) wooden dowel to bake them on. First use some waste clay to make holders for each end of the wooden dowel. This will help to keep the dowel from moving around. Cut the dowel down to 2" (5 cm) longer than the width of your bracelet piece. Powder the top side of the dowel well with cornstarch. Place the two holders, one at each end, under the dowel. Lay your bracelet strip or segments onto the powdered dowel. Gently press the bracelet strip or the segments against the top of the dowel, so that the segment is slightly curved to fit. Bake.

9. Remove from oven. If you have not cut your segments before baking, do so now, while the piece still is quite warm.

10. When cool, sand and buff each segment, using 320, 400, and 600 grit wet/dry sandpaper. Buff to a shine on a buffing wheel, or use 0000 steel wool to create a satin finish. Cut two lengths of cord, and thread each cord through the holes in the segments (Photo 4). Tie the ends together in a square knot, trim the ends, and then tug on the cord so that the knot slips into the hole in the segment next to it, so the knot won't show.

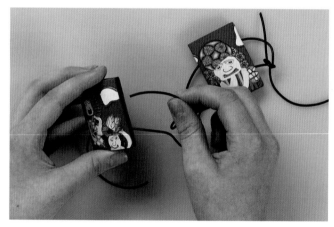

4. Stringing cord through the segments to assemble.

There you go. Slip the bracelet on your wrist, go shopping, and you are bound to hear some delightful comments about your piece of funky art. You can make a segmented bracelet using a wide variety of surface techniques such as transfers, silk screening, texturing, or other types of canework. Make pins to go with your bracelet, if you wish, from leftover clay.

FAUX CARVED IVORY JEWELRY

Designer
Dotty McMillan

I've always loved the look of old ivory beads. However, I know that none of us would want to use real ivory. In fact, it's pretty much illegal everywhere. After all, an elephant would have to give up its life in order for someone to use its tusks for such a project. We can achieve the rich look of aged ivory with polymer clay. If this necklace were real ivory, it would be quite heavy. With polymer it's remarkably lightweight. This is a very simple technique. Make extra beads for a matching bracelet if you wish.

MATERIALS

Polymer clay:

      Ecru/champagne, 4 oz (112 g)

      White, 2 oz (56 g)

      Translucent, 2 oz (56 g)

      Yellow, a pea-sized piece

Molds, a variety of fairly deep small round or oval shapes; silicone molds are the easiest to use, but any type will work

Polyester batting

Cornstarch or other mold release for molds that require it

Needle tool

Acrylic paint, burnt umber

Stiff paintbrush

Paper towel or terry cloth shop towel

Wet/dry sandpaper, 400 and 600 grits

Buffing wheel or a soft cotton cloth such as jeans material

Strong stringing material

Crimp beads for securing the stringing material

Filler beads (glass and sterling silver for the necklace pictured)

Clasps (optional)

1. To mix the ivory color, blend all the clays together until you get a soft beige color with a slight undertone of yellow. This is not a striated type of faux ivory. I have found that striations really don't show up well in these particular beads.

2. Roll a small ball of the ivory clay. Press it into one of the molds and remove it (Photo 1). Roll another ball of clay and do the same either with the same mold or with a different one. Place the two molded pieces together, back to back. Work with the edges so that the pieces are pretty much the same shape. If the two pieces when together are really flat, take them apart, roll out a very small snake of clay, and place it between the two molded pieces (Photo 2). Then gently press the sides around the snake of clay together. Be careful as you do all of this that your fingers do not flatten or remove the molded relief areas.

3. Use your needle tool to make a hole through the bead from end to end. Then go around the edges with the needle tool to make indentations, or to blend, or to do whatever you think looks good around the joined edges to camouflage them somewhat. Anything goes here, so don't get too picky. Don't take too long with each of these or you may diminish the carved appearance. Set your beads onto a pad of polyester batting, and bake.

1. A molded half-bead and its mold.

2. Two halves of a bead.

4. When the beads are cool, wet-sand them. Do not sand so hard that you sand off the raised areas of the bead. You just want to break the surface tension of the clay and smooth the raised areas some. Use a rather stiff paintbrush to apply burnt umber acrylic paint to a bead (Photo 3). Use a jabbing motion in order to get the paint into all of the recesses. Rub over the entire bead with your fingers. Check to make sure you haven't missed any areas.

5. Before the paint dries, begin wiping the excess paint off the bead. Use a paper towel or a terry cloth shop towel. After most of it is off, wash the paint off your hands. Now, take a look at the bead and see if you think it is too dark or needs to have more of the surface stain removed. Dampen the areas where you wish to remove more of the color and rub them with the towel or paper towel. Keep doing this until you are happy with the results. Let the paint in the recesses dry completely. Then buff the bead on a buffing wheel, or hand-buff it with a piece of soft cotton.

6. Lay out all of the ivory beads you have made and arrange them in a circle that pleases your artistic eye. Lay the filler beads into place to make sure you have enough. Once you like the way they are combined, string them, and fasten the ends using crimp beads. I prefer sterling silver crimp beads, which seem to be stronger than the base metal ones. They are not very expensive. If you make your string of beads long enough, you will not have to add a clasp, as it will fit over your head.

7. I've added a pendant to the necklace. It is also molded, but is larger and flatter than the beads and is one-sided. It is backed by a piece of black clay rolled out on the #3 setting (³⁄₃₂" or 2.4 mm) of the pasta machine. The front side is antiqued and finished in the same way as the beads.

8. Make a matching bracelet if you wish.

Now, why not make a necklace with all black beads antiqued with parchment white? Or how about trying jade antiqued with burnt sienna?

3. Applying the burnt umber.

PRECIOUS POD JADE NECKLACE

Designer
Dotty McMillan

These lightweight pod-shaped beads resemble large seed pods and are great fun to make and use. You can use almost any surface decoration you want: silk-screen, texture, photo transfer, cane slices, and more. For this project, you will make a large faux jade pod and slip it onto a sterling silver wire with metal and glass bead additions.

1. Mix ¼ of a pea-sized piece of orange clay into the green. This will desaturate the bright green and give it the look of many types of jade. If you feel the orange has made it too dark, add a bit more of the green. Or if it's still too bright, add a bit more orange. I like the look of the mica in the metallic green. Roll out a sheet of the jade clay on the #2 setting (⁷⁄₆₄" or 2.8 mm) of the pasta machine. Be sure the sheet is large enough to cut out at least two circles using the 2" (5 cm) cutter, but don't cut them yet.

2. Use the needle tool to draw decorations on the surface of the clay. Make good impressions, but do not cut through the clay completely. You can get the look of ancient Mexican art, rock art, ancient Chinese art, or just make doodles from your imagination. This really doesn't take much skill. Just have fun with it. If you don't like the finished piece, roll it out again and start over until you are happy with the results.

MATERIALS

Polymer clay:

       Premo! Sculpey metallic green, about 3 oz (84 g)

       Orange, small piece

       Waste clay, 8 oz (227 g)

Two old 100-watt light bulbs

Needle tool

Sharp blade

Plastic wrap, small sheet

Circle cutter, 2" (5 cm)

Sandpaper, 60 grit

Wet/dry sandpaper, 400 and 600 grits

Cyanoacrylate glue

Acrylic paint, parchment white

Stiff paintbrush

Pasta machine or acrylic roller

Small drill bit embedded in a polymer clay handle (see pages 82 to 83) or electric Dremel drill with a small bit

Buffing wheel or clay-compatible glaze

Small-gauge sterling silver neck ring (torque) with a friction or magnetic clasp

Miscellaneous beads with holes large enough to hold the silver neck ring

3. Lay a piece of plastic wrap over the top of the sheet, and then cut out two circles, using the 2" (5 cm) cutter. You have to press quite hard to get a complete cut. However, using the plastic wrap will help to bevel the edges nicely and will reduce the sanding time later.

4. Mix about 8 oz (227 g) of waste clay and make two small, round lumps with it. Flatten the bottoms so each stands straight. Press the screw end of each 100-watt light bulb into a lump of clay until it is in below the screw area; then snug the clay in close so the bulbs won't move when they are baked. Place one of the clay circles on top of each of the bulbs, and gently press them so that they conform to the rounded glass (Photo 1). Check to make sure you have not deformed the edges of the circle when doing this. Bake, let cool, and remove from the light bulbs.

1. One-half of a pod, ready to bake on its light bulb stand.

5. Place a piece of 60-grit sandpaper on your work surface and set one of the baked circles against it, domed side up. What you are going to do is to sand the bottom edges smooth and flat. Move the circle back and forth on the sandpaper, give it a quarter turn, and sand back and forth again (Photo 2). Do this all around the circle. Do the second circle the same way. Now hold the two circles together and check to see

2. Sanding the bottom of the pod half.

how they fit. What you want is a knife edge all around. If there are bumpy areas, use the sandpaper again until all the areas are flattened. If you have an electric Dremel tool with a small grinding bit, you can do this step much faster. Grind off most of the thick areas, and then finish up with a bit of sanding so that the bottom is completely flat.

6. Once the two pieces fit together nicely, place a small amount of cyanoacrylate glue around the edge of one of the pieces and then press the two pieces together. Make sure the fit is as good as possible. Let the glue set for an hour or so.

7. Use a stiff paintbrush to paint the entire surface of the pod bead with white acrylic paint. Use a jabbing movement to make sure the paint gets into all the recessed carved areas. Lightly wipe off the excess paint, trying not to disturb the paint that is in the carved areas. Let the paint dry thoroughly.

8. Sand the entire outside of the bead, using 400- and 600-grit wet/dry sandpaper. Buff to a high shine. If you don't have a buffing wheel, you can coat the sanded bead with any gloss glaze that is compatible with the clay.

3. Using a hand drill to drill holes for the neck ring.

9. Use a Dremel drill or a hand drill bit to drill holes through the beads for the neck ring (Photo 3).

10. Thread the pod and beads onto the silver neck ring in a pleasing arrangement. Now you have an elegant necklace to wear with your favorite outfit. How about making another piece using a different surface technique? What about black, gold, and silver mokume gane, as shown in the opener photo? How about bright cane slices or colorful graphic or photo transfers?

Pod beads can be used for making necklaces, bracelets, and pendants. For bracelets, you need to make very small pods. Pendants can be just about any size you want. You can make pods of various sizes or of all one size that can be strung as a necklace. For beads that are fairly small, you can use an inverted metal watercolor painter's pan, the kind with about 6 wells for holding paint. Just turn it upside down and lay your cut-out clay circles on top.

4. A variety of pod beads.

DRAGON SKIN TREASURE BOX

Designer
Dotty McMillan

Dark, rich, and mysterious, this dragon skin textured treasure box can hold jewelry, beads, loose change, and anything else you want to keep safe. Glints of gold evoke the era of knights and kings. These boxes make wonderful gifts and can be made in a wide variety of color combinations to suit everyone's taste. You'll find them quite simple to make. Once you've made one, you won't be able to stop.

MATERIALS

Polymer clay:

> Premo! Sculpey black, 2 oz (56 g)

> Premo! Sculpey gold, 2½ oz (70 g)

> Premo! Sculpey copper, 1 oz (28 g)

> Premo! Sculpey cadmium red, 1 oz (28 g)

> Liquid clay (optional)

> Waste clay, 2 oz (56 g)

Circle cookie cutters: 2¾", 1¾", 1½", and 1" (7, 4.3, 3.8, and 2.5 cm) diameters

Texture sheet; if possible, Shade-Tex Dots in a Grid, or other texture tool that will make raised dots

Several texture molds of any kind

Heavy-duty chipboard mailing tube, 2¾" (7 cm) diameter and 3" (7.5 cm) tall*

White glue such as Sobo glue

Sharp, wide blade

Small spray bottle with water

Pasta machine

Wet/dry sandpaper, 320, 400, and 600 grits

Buffing wheel or clay-compatible glaze

Cyanoacrylate glue

Palette knife

Old 60- or 70-watt light bulb with its screw-end embedded in a waste clay base and baked**

Colored or printed card stock

Most of these tubes come in 12" (30.5 cm) lengths and can be easily cut with a serrated knife.

**See page 111, Step 4.*

1. Coat the inside and outside of the mailing tube section with Sobo glue and let dry. Lightly sand around the inside edges of the top and bottom to get rid of any excess paper left from cutting the tube.

2. Roll out the black and all but 1 oz (28 g) of the gold clay on the widest setting of the pasta machine (⅛" or 3.2 mm). Set aside. Mix the copper and cadmium red clay together well, and then roll out. Cut the 3 sheets into rectangles that are all the same size, approximately 5" (12.7 cm) in width and 8½" (21.6 cm) in length. Stack the sheets together with the black on the bottom, the gold in the middle, and the copper/red on top. Press the sheets together firmly to remove any trapped air.

3. Roll all 3 stacked sheets through the pasta machine on the widest setting. Cut the sheet in half and stack with the same color on top of both pieces. Roll through the pasta machine again, cut, stack, and then repeat this once more (3 times in all).

4. Cut this long sheet in half and set one piece aside. If you are using the plastic texture sheet, spray it with water, and lay the black side of the clay against the sheet's concave side, not the convex side of the sheet. You want dots coming out on the clay, not going in. Run the sheet of clay and the texture sheet through the pasta machine together on the widest setting. Carefully remove the clay from the plastic sheet. If you are using another type of texture tool, texture the entire surface of the clay.

5. Using a very sharp blade, hold it at each end of the blade, parallel to the surface of the clay, and carefully shave off the tops of all the little raised dots or other raised pieces on the clay. Do this all over the entire sheet. You now have your dragon skin.

6. Repeat the entire process in Steps 4 and 5 with the second half of the long sheet, but this time start by placing the copper/red side of the clay against the texture sheet. You'll be surprised at the difference between the two sheets after they are textured and shaved.

7. Roll out the leftover 1 oz of gold clay, and texture the surface using a mold or any other fairly deep texturing tool. Cut out two 1¾" (4.3 cm) circles of gold and set them aside.

8. Cut various widths of each of the sheets of textured dragon skin that are the height of the tube (3"), and begin placing them in a pleasing array around the chipboard tube (Photo 1). When the tube is completely covered, place the two gold clay circles on opposite sides of the tube, over the dragon skin.

1. Adding strips of clay around the tube.

9. Cut out two 1" (2.5 cm) circles from either of the sheets of dragon skin and center them on top of the gold circles (you can see this in Photo 4). Cut two 1½" (3.8 cm) wide strips of the red-sided sheet of clay, and place them on either side of the gold circles as a belt. Cut the ends of the strips to fit around the circle by using the 1¾" (4.3 cm) cutter. Snug all the seams together so that none of the chipboard tube shows.

10. Roll out the waste clay into a sheet that is about 4" × 7" (10 × 17.8 cm). Cut the leftover dragon skin into various-sized squares and cover the waste clay sheet with them. Be sure that the seams are snugged well together. Roll the two together through the pasta machine on the widest setting of the machine. This smoothes out the textured sheet and opens and spreads out the pattern of small dots (Photo 2).

11. Use a circle cutter to cut out two 2¾" (7 cm) circles from the patterned sheet you just created, and set these pieces aside. Cut out one 3¼" (8.3 cm) circle, center it on top of the light bulb, and carefully smooth it to fit the curve of the bulb. From the remaining pieces of the textured clay, cut out and add several smaller circles and then add a small twisted top piece

2. Smoothed out dragon skin pieces after going through pasta machine.

to the center of the top (Photo 3). This is the domed lid for your box. Bake the clay on the light bulb. Use a small palette knife to remove the clay from the bulb.

12. Use one 2¾" (7 cm) circle for the bottom of your box. If you have some liquid clay, place a coating along the bottom edges of the box, and carefully fit the circle to it. Set the box onto your baking surface with the bottom side down. This will ensure that the bottom will bake in place and adhere correctly. Make sure the circle is evenly centered against the box bottom. If you do not have access to liquid clay to adhere it, you can use some very soft black clay instead. Bake the box and let cool.

13. Sand and buff the box and the lid. Don't sand so much that you remove all the bumpiness on the box portion. This is part of the charm of this technique.

3. Making the top, adding decorations.

Just hit each area with a 400- and a 600-grit paper about 6 or 7 times. That's it. The lid won't be bumpy except for the added circles. Buff it the same as way you did the box.

14. Sand and buff the second 3¼" (8.3 cm) circle. You now need to make a plug or flange for the bottom of the lid, so that the lid will stay in place. To do this, roll out waste clay on the #1 setting of the pasta machine, and fold in half so there are two layers. Roll out any remaining pieces of the dragon skin and lay it on top of the waste clay to make a third layer. If you do not have enough of the patterned clay, just use plain gold clay, as in the photo. Cut a circle from the 3 layers of clay that will just fit inside the opening of the box. Bake the plug and let cool. Sand and buff the top and sides. Glue the plug to the 3¼" (8.3 cm) baked circle.

15. Place the sandpaper on your work surface and sand the bottom of the domed lid until its bottom edges are nice and flat. Glue the domed lid to the top of the 3¼" (8.3 cm) circle.

16. Line the inside of the box with commercial card stock, or if you have a computer and printer, print your own design for the lining on heavy-duty matte photo quality paper. Cut the lining to fit, and coat the back with white glue. Fit smoothly inside the box.

Your treasure box is now ready to use. The exterior of this box can also be made using mokume gane, silk screening, cane slices, and any other technique that you like.

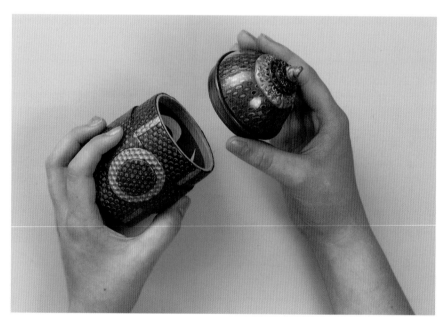

4. The finished container, showing the plug on the top, here made of gold clay.

DECORATIVE KNOBS

Designer
Dotty McMillan

hat fun it can be to fancy up your chest of drawers, kitchen cabinets, jewelry boxes, and inside doors with these delightful drawer and doorknobs. There's no limit here to the design possibilities. They can be made with shimmering pastels, bold crayon colors, fancy florals, gilded textures; you name it, it will probably work.

MATERIALS

Polymer clay:

> Premo! Sculpey or Kato Polyclay: pearl, 2 oz (56 g)

> Premo! Sculpey: alizarin crimson, small amounts

> Liquid clay such as Liquid Sculpey (preferred) or a good-quality white glue

Super Copper Pearl-Ex mica powder or other copper mica powder

Purchased wooden knob in the size you wish, with proper-sized screw

Clay-compatible glaze

Sharp blade

Pasta machine or acrylic roller

Small triangle-shaped cutter

Circle cookie cutters

Mold made from a small, fancy button

14K gold Krylon pen (optional)

Metallic copper acrylic paint (optional)

1. Coat the top and outside edge of the wooden knob with Liquid Sculpey or white glue. If you are using white glue, let it dry completely.

2. Choose a circle cutter that is about ¼" (0.6 cm) larger accross than the top of your knob. You may need to experiment with some waste clay to find the right size. If you can't find a cutter that works well, you can draw a circle of the right size on card stock and cut it out to use as a template.

3. You will need to mix 3 shades of pearl clay for this knob. To do this, use one-half of the pearl clay and add a half of a pea-sized amount of the crimson clay. Mix until it is all one shade. What you want is a medium to light pinkish color to cover the knob. Cut the amount of remaining pearl clay in half. To one-half, mix in red clay until it is about 3 shades darker than the first clay you mixed. Add enough red clay to the other half of the pearl clay to make an even darker red.

4. Roll out all 3 shades of the clay on the #1 (⅛" or 3.2 mm) setting of the pasta machine. Using the lightest shade of clay, cut out a circle that is the right size to cover the top of your wooden knob as well as extend down under the edge of the top for about ⅛" (3 mm). Gently ease the circle onto the knob top, smoothing it into place, and turn it under at the edge. This will ensure that the clay will never come off the knob (Photo 1).

5. Using the next-darkest shade of the clay, cut a second circle from the clay you rolled on the #1 setting of the pasta machine; it should be about half the diameter of the first circle. Center this circle on top of the first clay circle you used to cover the knob.

6. Use the darkest shade of the clay to make a molded piece with the fancy button mold. (You can use waste clay to make this mold, or a silicone compound, or some Super Elasticlay. See pages 21 to 24.) Place the molded piece on top of the other two on the knob. Photo 2 shows the pieces for the doorknob top.

7. With any remaining dark or medium dark clay, cut out a number of tiny triangles (Photo 2) and space them evenly around the edge of the second circle and around the edge of the molded piece.

8. Using your fingertip, gently gild the top of the molded piece and all of the triangles with Super Copper Pearl-Ex Mica Powder; any other copper mica powder may be substituted.

9. Bake the knob and let cool. When cool, glaze the clay portions with several coats of a clay-compatible glaze. This will help protect it from the touch of the many fingers it will encounter in use.

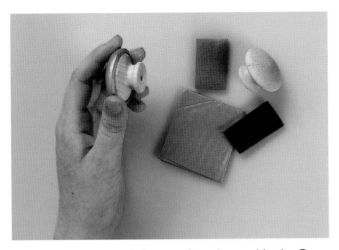

1. Light pink mixture of clay was shaped around knob. On table, uncovered doorknob plus swatches of all three colors: two pinks and a red.

2. Pieces of clay to decorate knob, silicone mold for making decorations, and a molded decoration.

Optional: To give the knob a very nice finished look, paint the back with metallic copper acrylic paint, and touch the top of the molded piece here and there with the gold pen.

Variations: Try different colors and shades of colors, using the plain pearl Premo! Sculpey or Kato pearl clay as the base color. The pearl always results in a wonder-ful, luminous effect that will enhance just about anything. Or go with bright crayon colors for a child's room or craft room. For the bedroom, use a flower cane that matches your wallpaper, bedspread, or curtains. The flower cane and leaf cane are perfect for these (see pages 45 and 46). They can be made any color you wish.

3. The finished knob.

ELEGANT FAN & LIGHT PULLS

Designer
Dotty McMillan

There is nothing more blah than seeing a long cord or chain hanging down from an overhead light or ceiling fan. It just hangs there, looking thin and sad. But add a fancy tassel pull and Voila! Instant magic! It gives you something solid to grip that feels good. These pulls are very simple to make yet extremely effective.

ARTFUL WAYS WITH POLYMER CLAY

MATERIALS

Polymer clay, black, 3 oz (84 g)

Wooden dowel, ¾" (1.9 cm) wide, 8" (20.3 cm) long

Cord or buna-N rubber cord, 1 or 2 mm (1/32" or 1/16") diameter or ball chain, 4" (10 cm) length

Mold from a metal filigree piece or other item to make a nice surface pattern

Readymade tassel 4" to 5" long (10 to 12.7 cm), or yarns to make one, or beads for a beaded tassel

Pasta machine

Super Bronze Pearl-Ex mica powder or equivalent

Needle tool

Thin knitting needle

Wet/dry sandpaper, 400 grit

Buffing wheel

Clay-compatible glaze

Cyanoacrylate glue

Cornstarch

Jar lid or acrylic plastic square, 3 × 3" (7.5 × 7.5 cm)

1. Wrapping clay around a dowel.

2. Trimming the molded black decoration.

1. Roll out the black clay on the #1 setting (⅛" or 3.2 mm) of the pasta machine. Cut out a rectangle that is 2" tall and 5" wide (5 × 12.5 cm), or at least wide enough to fit around the dowel with some extra. Lightly powder one surface of the rectangle with cornstarch, except for ¼" (6 mm) on one of the short ends. Place the powdered side against the dowel, and wrap the clay completely around (Photo 1). Trim off the excess so the clay fits around the dowel, and butt the unpowdered clay ends tightly together. Leave the clay tube on the dowel.

2. Roll out another sheet of black clay about 5" × 5". Powder and press the sheet into the filigree mold or other texturing object and remove. Cut 2 squares from the molded black clay, each 2" × 2" (5 × 5 cm); see Photo 2. Place one textured clay square on each side of the tube on the dowel. Make sure each is

firmly pressed against the clay tube. Carefully remove the entire tube from the dowel. Use your fingertip to gild the raised edges of the molded square with the bronze powder. Try to avoid getting it in the recesses.

3. To make the bicone for the top, roll a ball of black clay that is the same diameter as the tube. Use a square of clear acrylic plastic or a flat smooth lid from a jar to roll a bicone shape. (See page 53 and opener photo for reference.) You want a slightly flat bicone rather than a tall one. Fit this piece firmly on top of the clay tube. You may have to adjust the size and shape to fit your tube.

4. If you are using a ball chain, then you must embed it into the clay at the top of the bicone. Be sure you bury at least two or more of the little balls in the clay. A chain is a good idea if you plan to attach the pull to the same type of chain on your fan or overhead light. If you are using the cord, use a needle tool to make a hole through the bicone into the open area of the tube. Enlarge the hole a little with a knitting needle or wooden skewer. Stand the tube on its flat end and bake.

5. When the piece is cool, wet-sand and buff the top bicone only. If you have a chain embedded, be sure to hold it securely so that it doesn't get tangled in the buffing wheel. You could use a clay-compatible glaze instead of buffing.

6. If you are not using a chain, make a small loop of cord or buna-N rubber cord, and fit into the hole on top of the light pull. If the hole is too small, drill it out with a drill bit. Add a small amount of cyanoacrylate glue to the end of the cord and reinsert into the hole. Let the glue dry.

7. Coat the textured pieces on the sides of the tube, which are gilded with bronze mica powder, with a clay-compatible glaze.

8. If you are using a ready-made tassel, coat the top of it with glue and insert into the bottom of the pull (Photo 3). Let sit for several hours. Then your pull is ready to attach to a fan or light.

9. If you can't locate the right size tassel, make your own using interesting yarn. Simply wrap the yarn around a piece of cardboard that is 5" long (12.7 cm) or more. Make as many wraps as necessary to form a tassel the thickness you need to insert into the bottom of the pull (Photo 4). Thread a piece of carpet thread underneath one end of the wrapped yarn and tie snugly. Remove the yarn from the cardboard and, holding it firmly at the top with one hand, cut through all the bottom loops. Glue and insert the tied end into the bottom of the pull.

3. Inserting a tassel in a finished cover.

4. Making a tassel (left) and a finished tassel (right).

This is quite a large pull. You can vary the size by using a different diameter dowel. Instead of the filigree molded surface, you could use graphic transfers. Put the transfers onto the two squares before applying them to the surface of the tube. Or use the dragon skin mokume gane technique. Use black clay as a base, cut out two squares of the dragon skin, and apply. Vary the color and make an ivory-colored pull, as shown in the opener photo. The surface techniques for these pulls are endless.

RING-A-DING NECKLACE

Designer
Dotty McMillan

This is one of my favorite styles of necklace and one that is such fun to make. It is ideal for just about any surface technique you can think of. For the necklace pictured I have used textured surfaces, textured and gilded surfaces, caned pieces, and a few other techniques. It can be made in any color combination that you prefer, so pick colors that appeal to you. This one is done in pinkish orange, yellow, and light pearl green, with black accents here and there.

MATERIALS

Polymer clay:

      Main color choice, 4 oz (112 g)

      Secondary color choice, 4 oz (112 g)

      Third complementary color, 2 oz (56 g)

      Contrasting color (such as black), 2 oz (56 g)

Short pieces of wooden dowels in at least 3 diameters: ⅝", ¾", 1½" (1.6, 1.9, and 3.8 cm)

Plastic texture sheets or other texture tools

Clay-compatible glaze

Sharp blade

Needle tool

Pasta machine or acrylic roller

Mica powders in gold or copper or others that suit your color choices

Stringing material

Clasp

This necklace is actually two in one. There is one main string that holds very small caned beads, large bicone-shaped beads, and round beads. Ring beads with large openings go over the main string in places and have some small beads inside their large holes. Very wide striped dangly ring beads go over the inner string of beads. Some of the round beads and bicones act as stops, while others nestle in the ends of the ring beads. If you look closely at the opening photo, you will be able to see how this is done.

1. Divide each of the 3 clay colors except the contrasting one into two parts, with one-third of each color for one part, and two-thirds of each color for the other part. Set the one-third parts of each aside. Use the two-third parts of each to make a cane. This can be just about any simple cane. A bulls-eye cane with triangle pieces added, such as is shown in Photo 1, is easy and works well. Reduce the cane down to about ½" (1.3 cm) in diameter. Cut it in half. Reduce one-half to ⁵⁄₁₆" (0.8 cm). Set both cane sizes aside. These will make the small beads and also decorate the larger beads.

1. Creating a cane with triangle pieces, using the 3 colors.

2. Use the other pieces (one-third parts) of each color separately. Roll a sheet of the main color on the #3 setting (³⁄₃₂" or 2.4 mm) of the pasta machine. Texture the sheet using a plastic texture sheet, rubber stamp, mold, or any other texture tool. Cut a long strip of clay that is 1" (2.5 cm) wide. Use one of the dowels to wrap and measure the clay, and cut the clay the size you need to make a tube bead that is the same diameter of the dowel. Remove the strip from the dowel and slip it on a finger. Use another finger to press and seal the seam (Photo 2). While the bead is still on your finger, gently gild the raised portion with mica powder. Use the pad of your fingertip for this. Do the same thing with all 3 colors, making 6 textured ring beads in all (or more for a longer necklace). Bake and cool.

2. Sealing the seam on a textured tube bead. On table, texture mold.

3. With the colors left after you make the ring beads, make a variety of other shapes of beads. Make 5 or 6 round beads of various sizes, using cane slices on the surface, and/or scraps of various leftover colors. Make 3 or 4 bicone beads using cane slices on the surface. Make 4 or 5 dangly striped rings by twisting snakes of a few colors of clay into rings that are 1¾" and 1" (4.3 and 2.5 cm) in diameter (see Photo 3).

3. Closeup of necklace shows reduced canes in little beads and in some other beads.

4. Retrieve the other half of the canes you made originally, which you rolled down to small sizes (½" and ⁵⁄₁₆"). Slice off pieces that are ¼" wide (6 mm) or slightly thicker. These will be the small beads (see Photo 3). You will need a lot of these, so slice the entire cane. Pierce each slice through the rounded outside (not through the image), with a needle tool, and bake them.

5. If you want shiny beads, glaze them with a clay-compatible glaze. Be sure to glaze the gilded beads to protect their surfaces.

6. You are now ready to string the beads you have created. A bead board will be extremely helpful. If you don't have one, lay out your beads on a large, smooth work surface that has no slant. There is no strict rule on the stringing sequence. Each end should have a number of the small beads so that it is comfortable on your neck. Add a bicone next to these. Then string alternating beads. Use small beads inside the large-hole ring beads. Add round beads here and there. Add a few small dangly striped rings on the sides, and 2 or 3 at the center. Hold the piece up now and then to see how it hangs. When you are satisfied with the arrangement, add the clasp.

Have some beads left over? Hang on to them. You can add them to another necklace. Try other surface techniques such as silk-screened rings, which are beautiful.

TALL TEAPOT

Designer
Dotty McMillan

This whimsical teapot is ornamental only; it can't hold tea. However, it can hold tons of other things such as those pesky pennies that are forever multiplying, or dried flowers, or buttons, or beads. You get the idea.

The instructions are for a puzzle-type design, which you make piece by piece as you go. A teapot could be made with many other designs or colors. Make it funky, make it serene; this tall vessel is adaptable to just about any style.

MATERIALS

Polymer clay*:

> Kato Polyclay black, 2 oz (56 g)

> Kato Polyclay red, 8 oz (227 g)

> Kato Polyclay white, 2 oz (56 g)

Kemper triangle cutter, medium size (¾", or 1.9 cm); optional

Smallest Kemper circle cutter or brass tube ³⁄₁₆" (0.5 cm) wide

Heavy-duty mailing tube, 10" (25 cm) length or longer, 2½" (6.4 cm) diameter

White glue

Set of circle cutters, including 3" (7.6 cm) and 2½" (6.4 cm) circle cutters

Wax paper

Texture sheets, rubber stamps, or other texture tools

Sharp blade

Craft knife

Narrow paintbrush or chopstick

Cyanoacrylate glue

Wet/dry sandpaper, 320 and 400 grits

Buffing wheel or soft cotton cloth, or clay-compatible glaze

Pasta machine and acrylic roller

Sheet of decorative paper for lining teapot (optional)

75-watt light bulb, baked into a base of waste clay (see page 111)

Polyester batting

Small face mold (optional)

Ruler

Oven that holds an object 10" (25 cm) in length with at least 1" clearance at each end

*Kato Polyclay is preferred (it works extremely well for the canes); however, other clays can be used.

1. Cut the mailing tube to a 10" (25.4 cm) length if it is longer. Coat the outside of the tube with white glue and set aside to dry. While the tube is drying, make one black-and-white ¾" (1.9 cm) diameter jelly roll cane for the top, one black-and-white double jelly roll cane, and one black-and-white candy-stripe snake. Twist and roll the snake down to about ¼" (0.6 cm) in diameter. You will need two lengths of this snake of about 11" (28 cm) each. Also make one red-and-white striped loaf cane and one black-and-white-wrapped translucent cane that is about 1" (2.5 cm) square. See cane instructions with this project to make these canes. Put the canes aside to set up for easier slicing.

2. To make the lid, roll out a sheet of black clay on the widest setting (⅛" or 3.2 mm) of the pasta machine or use a roller. Cut out a 3" (7.6 cm) circle from the black using a circle cutter. Center the black circle on top of the light bulb. With the palm of your hand, slowly and carefully mold the clay to fit the top of the bulb like a cap. The warmth of your hand will help to compress and snug the clay against the glass. Be sure all areas of the clay are touching the surface of the bulb.

3. Reduce one of the black-and-white candy-cane snakes so it is about ⅛" (0.3 cm) thick and wrap it around the edge of the black circle on the light bulb (Photo 1). Trim away the excess snake, and fit its ends together.

1. Making the top of the teapot on the light bulb.

4. Roll out a small sheet of red clay and texture it using a small-patterned texture sheet, rubber stamp, or other texturing tool. Cut out 8 to 10 triangles with the triangle tool or a blade from the red clay, and space them evenly above the candy cane snake on the black clay on the light bulb.

5. Take thin slices of the single black-and-white jelly roll cane that is rolled to about ½" (1.3 cm) diameter, and place them above and between the red triangles on the lid. You can see the finished lid in Photo 4.

6. Take a ¼" (0.6 cm) slice of the jelly roll cane, and center it on top of the lid. It should stand on its side. Press to ensure that it is in good contact with the black clay. Cut out a black clay 2½" (6.4 cm) circle that is rolled out on the thickest pasta machine setting. Bake along with the piece on the light bulb, but separately. After they are baked, remove the lid from the light bulb and glue the circle onto the bottom of the lid with cyanoacrylate glue. Set the lid aside for now.

7. Wrap a black-and-white candy stripe snake around the bottom edge of the mailing tube. It should be about ¼" thick. Trim, and fit the ends together. Add a row of black-and-white double jelly roll slices around the base of the tube above the candy stripe (Photo 2). Add a row of the translucent cane slices, each of which is backed with a thin square of red clay, above the jelly roll row. The red will glow through the translucent clay after the piece is finished (see Photo 4 for reference).

2. Adding double jelly roll canes to the base of the cardboard tube.

8. Roll out a 3" × 11" (7.6 × 28 cm) long sheet of red clay and one the same size of black clay on the #3 setting (3⁄32" or 2.4 mm) of the pasta machine. Set the black sheet aside. Use the smallest Kemper circle cutter or a narrow brass tube, and cut holes over the entire sheet of red clay (Photo 3). Do not get the holes too close together. Keep the holes at least ¼" away from the outside edges. Working on a piece of waxed paper, lay the sheet of black clay on top of the red sheet and gently press together to make sure there is no trapped air. Gently remove the piece from the waxed paper and wrap it around the tube, red side out, just above the row of translucent canes. Trim to fit. Add a row of double jelly roll cane slices around the top of the black-and-red sheet.

3. Cutting holes in red clay with a very small cutter.

9. Now comes the fun part! Texture a sheet of red clay and one of black. Use various textures on each sheet, perhaps a plastic texture sheet, rubber stamp, or other texture tool. Make some slices from the translucent cane, back the slices with squares of red clay, and make some slices from the red-and-white striped loaf cane.

10. Begin cutting and fitting pieces together around the teapot. Make and place some cuts from the textured clay, and fit some of the cane slices beside them. Add pieces as if it were a puzzle. You can follow what I have done on my teapot or just go off on your own

and fit pieces together in a way that appeals to you.

11. To make the spout and the handle, roll out one short log that is narrow at one end and thick at the other and one long snake that is tapered at each end from red clay. The length and diameter of these depend on how you want your spout and handle to look. The ones on my teapot are quite simple. You can make them more elaborate if you like. Use the handle end of a paintbrush or a chopstick to create the opening in the spout. You can add a narrow textured strip around the base of the spout where it is attached to the tube, to help secure the attachment.

12. After you attach the spout and the handle onto the teapot, lay the teapot down on a thick bed of polyester batting on a baking surface. Use extra polyester batting under the spout and handle to make certain they do not slump or move in baking. Bake the teapot on the polyester batting at the temperature recommended by the clay manufacturer. Let cool in the oven. You will find some of the polyester batting attached to one side of the teapot. However, it is easy to pluck it off. Go over it several times to make sure you have it all removed.

13. To add to the whimsical feel of the pot, I added a tiny molded face and a hand-formed hand. You may have other ideas that will give yours the look that you want.

14. To make the bottom piece (foot) of the teapot, lay out scraps left from cane slices and make a sheet of them using the widest setting on the pasta machine. Cut a 3" (7.6 cm) circle from the sheet. Bake. Once the piece is cool, attach it to the bottom of the tube using some cyanoacrylate glue. It will be slightly larger than the tube, which will help stabilize the teapot when it is standing.

15. For the flange on the bottom of the lid, which will hold it in place, use scrap clay rolled out on the widest setting of the pasta machine. Stack together about 4 scrap sheets, each large enough for cutting out a 2½" circle. Use any canes you have left, make a sheet of these on the #3 (3⁄32" or 2.4 mm) setting of the pasta machine, and add this sheet to the top of the 4-sheet stack. Cut through all 5 layers with the 2½" cutter. Bake. The flange may have a slightly larger diameter than the opening of the teapot. You can carefully trim it around the edge to fit. Be careful not to make it too small. If it is still too large after baking, use rough sandpaper to narrow it to fit, and finish with 400-grit sand-

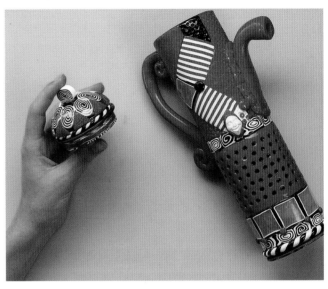

4. The lid, with layered flange. At right: a finished teapot.

paper. Once it is the correct size, attach the flange to the bottom of the lid with cyanoacrylate glue (Photo 4).

16. Once your teapot is done, you can either leave it as is or glaze it with a clay-compatible glaze. An alternative is to wet-sand it using the 320- and 400-grit sandpapers and then buff it using a soft cotton cloth or a buffing wheel.

17. I always line the inside of my teapots with colorful card stock or with a lining I design on the computer, printed out on heavyweight matte photo paper. The lining is glued inside the pot with white glue.

Once you make one of these teapots, you can use just about any design you wish to create more.

CANES FOR TALL TEAPOT PROJECT

SINGLE JELLY ROLL CANE. A single jelly roll cane is made by layering a white and a black sheet (made on the #1 setting of the pasta machine, each ⅛" thick) together, running them back through the pasta machine on the #1 setting, and then, starting at one end, rolling the layers up. The cane can then be rolled down to whatever size is needed. We need ¾" (1.9 cm) diameter (Photo 1).

DOUBLE JELLY ROLL CANE. A double jelly roll cane is made by layering a white and a black sheet (made on the #1 setting, each ⅛" thick) and running them back through the pasta machine on the #1 setting. Roll the sheet up from both ends, but roll one end with the black clay on the outside (see Photo 1) and the other end with the white clay on the outside. Roll until you have about 1½" (3.8 cm) of the unrolled

1. Above, single (far right) and double jelly roll cane (left and near right). In center, start of candy stripe cane. Bottom, cutting slices from a square wrapped translucent cane.

sheet left in between the two rolls. Make 3 folds in the unrolled portion, and snug the 2 jelly roll portions against the fold (see Photo 1). The cane should end up about ½" (1.3 cm) × 1½" (3.8 cm).

CANDY STRIPE SNAKE. Roll out a black snake to about 1" in diameter. Roll a white snake of the same size. Snug the two snakes together and begin by twisting them a little. Lay the piece down on your work surface and hold one end of it with one hand. With the other hand roll the other end away from you. Straighten the piece out, flip it end over end, and roll and twist again. Adjust the twists now and then to even them out. Also, straighten and roll the whole piece now and then to smooth out the snake. Twist and roll down to about ¼" diameter (Photo 1). You will need about 22" (56 cm) of this candy-stripe snake.

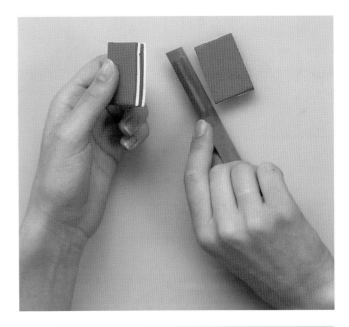

SQUARE TRANSLUCENT CANE. Make a translucent cane by first rolling a translucent log about 2" (5 cm) in diameter. Then wrap the log with a sheet of white clay rolled on the pasta machine on the #5 setting (¹⁄₁₆" or 1.6 mm). Wrap the log again with a sheet of black clay rolled on the #5 setting. Roll to smooth; then use an acrylic roller to shape the log into a rectangular solid with square side faces (see Photo 1).

STRIPED LOAF CANE. Roll out a sheet of red clay and a sheet of white on the #1 setting. Cut each sheet to about 3½" (9 cm) square. Stack the two sheets together, pressing gently to make sure there is no trapped air. Cut the stack in half and stack it again (Photo 2). Repeat this again until you have about 16 stripes. You can see these on the top half of the teapot body. The side of the cane is about 1¾" (4.4 cm) square.

2. Making a striped loaf cane by cutting and layering red and white pieces.

COOKIE CUTTER CONTAINER

Designer
Dotty McMillan

I'm always taking my rings off whenever I do the dishes, work on the computer, or play with clay. I set them down and am forever looking for them later. I'm lucky that so far I haven't lost any of them. I decided to create some solutions to this bad habit: ornate little jars made using a set of circular cookie cutters. Now I keep one of these at every spot where I usually shed my rings. I just pop them into the jar, put on the lid, and now I know exactly where they are when I want them again. Fast and easy to make, these jars can be used to hold just about any small items you might have.

1. Thoroughly mix 2½ oz (70 g) of the translucent clay with a pea-sized piece of opaque orange and half that much of the cadmium yellow. Using the pasta machine to mix saves time and hands. You want to get a nice, fairly translucent peachy-orange color.

2. Roll out the new color on the #1 (⅛" or 3.2 mm) setting of the pasta machine. Your piece should be about 2½" × 6½" (6.4 cm × 16.5 cm). If you are using a texture sheet, spray the sheet with water, place the piece of clay against one side of it, and then run both through the pasta machine on the #1 setting, with the clay side away from you. If you are using some other method of texturing, be sure the entire surface of the piece is textured. Trim the clay to measure 2" × 5½" (5 cm × 14 cm).

MATERIALS

Polymer clay:

  Translucent, 4½ oz (126 g)

  Opaque orange, cadmium yellow, and green: ½ oz (14 g) each

  Liquid clay

Plastic texture sheets or other texturing items

Small commercial decorative flexible mold. Fleur de lis is nice (or make your own mold)

Tiny ball-tipped stylus

Set of circular cookie cutters, including sizes 2", 1¾" and 1½" (5, 4.4, and 3.8 cm)

Mold of a small, ornate button

Pasta machine or acrylic roller

Painter's palette knife

14K gold acrylic pen (optional)

Needle tool

Extruder such as clay gun (optional)

Armorall

Clay-compatible glaze

14K Krylon gold acrylic pen (optional)

Spray bottle with water

3. Turn the 1¾" (4.4 cm) circle cutter upside down so that the rolled metal edge is on the bottom. Wrap the clay piece you just cut around the outside of the cutter, making sure that the bottom edge of the clay rests on top of the rolled edge of the cutter. Trim and butt the clay edges together securely. You want to make a cylinder about 2" tall.

4. To 1 oz (28 g) of plain translucent clay, add a half-pea-sized piece of the opaque green clay. Mix well. To 1 oz of translucent clay, add a half-pea-sized piece of yellow. Mix well so there is no variation in color throughout.

5. It's time to decorate your little container using the green clay and leftover orange clay. The sky's the limit here. Go as ornate as you like or as plain as you want. Use the flexible mold to make some decorative pieces. Use an extruder or roll out strings of clay by hand, which you can curl and twist and add to the piece. Roll tiny balls of clay and indent them with the ball-tipped stylus. Texture the clay and cut little circles, squares, triangles, etc. to apply to the container (Photo 1). When finished decorating, bake the cylinder on the cutter and let cool.

1. Decorating the container.

6. When cool, coax the cylinder of clay off the cutter using a small painter's palette knife, like removing a cake from a pan. Using some Armorall on the blade is helpful.

7. For the jar top or lid, cut 3 circles from peachy orange clay, one each of 2" (5 cm), 1¾" (4.4 cm), and 1½" (3.8 cm). Stack these 3 pieces together with the smaller circles on top. Use a mold made from a small, ornate button to mold a piece to go on top of these three pieces. Add small balls of clay on top for decoration.

8. Run the remaining peachy orange clay through the pasta machine on the #1 setting. Fold it in half, and then cut a circle using the 1½" (3.8 cm) cutter. Center this on the bottom of the jar top. It will act as a stop to keep the lid from sliding off.

9. Roll out another small sheet of peachy orange clay on the #1 setting and cut out a 2" (5 cm) circle. This is the bottom piece for your container. Place this circle on the bottom of the cylinder, using some liquid clay to help it adhere. Add feet to the bottom if you want (Photo 3).

10. Roll a snake of the orange clay that is about ¼" (0.6 cm) in diameter and long enough to fit around the edge of the container. Use a needle tool to make indentations along the length of the snake if you like. Fit this piece around the lower edge of the cylinder. Check to make sure that the top for the container fits well on the cylinder and that the piece added as a stop will fit inside the

cylinder. Photo 2 shows a side view of a lid. Re-bake the container and bake the lid (separately), and let cool.

11. Give the entire piece a coat of clay-compatible glaze. If you want to jazz the piece up some, use a 14K gold acrylic pen here and there to accent.

Now, go ahead and make more little jars to hold precious things, in other colors. The opening photo shows some possibilities. Use pearl clay as your base and add various colors to it for a satiny look. You'll find them handy to have around, as well as to give for gifts.

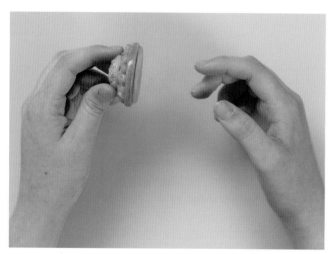

2. Side view of lid, showing stop.

3. Bottoms of two containers, one with feet.

SILK-SCREENED CLOCK

Designer
Dotty McMillan

The small size of this wall clock makes it easy to hang just about anyplace in the house. In my small studio, with limited wall space, it works perfectly. The instructions here are for a rich silk-screened surface, but you can use almost any technique. A clock that is made with canes is shown at the left in this photo.

MATERIALS

Premo! Sculpey polymer clay:

      Black, 5 oz (140 g)

      Gold pearl, 1½ oz (42 g)

      Copper pearl, 1½ oz (42 g)

      Waste clay, 3 oz (84 g)

Acrylic paint: black, metallic gold, and metallic copper

Old CD disk

Clock works (battery-type, with wall hanger)

Paintbrush

Battery for clock

Small-patterned silk screens and squeegee

Ruler

Blade or craft knife

Needle tool

Cyanoacrylate glue

Pasta machine or roller

Wet/dry sandpaper, 400 and 600 grits

Wax paper

Buffing equipment (optional)

1. Make 5 or 6 small silk screens, using one of the methods you prefer (see pages 32-35 for directions). Use small overall repeat patterns.

2. Once your screens are done, roll out all but 1½ oz (42 g) of the waste clay on the #3 setting (3/32" or 2.4 mm) of the pasta machine. Cut it into a square that is 5½" × 5½" (14 × 14 cm) and lay it out on your work surface. Place an old CD down on top of the clay, and mark the outline and the center of it with a needle tool (Photo 1). Remove the CD and set aside.

1. Marking the outline with a needle tool.

3. Roll the black, gold, and copper clay on the #2 setting (7/64" or 2.8 mm) of the pasta machine or the equivalent thickness. Cut the sheets into rectangles that are 2" × 2½" (5 × 6 cm).

4. Using the silk screens you've made, screen the paint onto all the pieces of the 3 colors of clay according to the directions on pages 32 to 34. Use black paint on the gold clay and on the copper clay. Use gold and copper paint on the black clay. Let the paint dry completely.

5. Cut out small strips, blocks, etc. of all the colors of screened clay and fit them together in a random pattern to completely cover and overlap by at least ¼" (0.6 cm) the CD outline you traced on the waste sheet of clay (Photo 2). Play with the shapes until you are happy with the layout. Carefully snug the seams of the pieces together. Don't press too hard on the painted areas, because the paint can easily peel off until it is baked.

6. Place the assembled silk-screened sheet of clay face up onto a piece of wax paper. Center the CD disk on top of the clay, and use a craft knife to trim the clay around the CD edges to make the clock face. Mark the center hole. Remove the CD, and bake the clock face piece. The silk-

2. Assembling the silk-screened clay pieces.

screened paint is now bonded with the clay and is very durable. You now have two sheets of clay joined together; the waste clay is on the bottom and the silk-screened clay is on top.

7. When the clock face is cool, wet-sand all around the edges. If you have access to a buffing wheel, buff the edges to a nice shine. Do not sand or buff the silk-screened area.

8. You can make numbers in various ways or not add them at all. Simple black ovals at the 12, 3, 6, and 9 o'clock spots work well. For the sample clock, I added simple numbers around the outside at 4 places. If you prefer, you can usually buy clock numbers from the same supplier you used to get your clock works. To make the numbers pictured, I rolled out 4 thin snakes of black clay and bent them into the

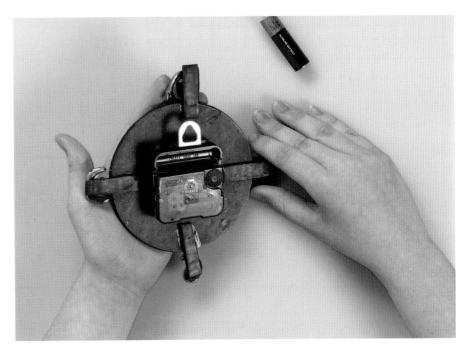

3. Back of clock, showing clock mechanism and strips of clay for numbers.

shape of the numbers. These are attached to narrow strips of black clay that are glued to the back of the clock with cyanoacrylate glue (Photo 3). I used metallic gold paint to illuminate the numbers.

9. Assemble the clockworks according to the manufacturer's directions. Drill a hole through the center of the clock face in the size needed to insert the clockworks. After inserting the works, add the minute hands and install the clock batteries; your clock is up and run-

ning. Most commercial clockworks come with an attachment for hanging the clock.

The round shape of the CD invites one to make a cat face clock, cutting out features from various colors of clay. The clock is also beautiful when the surface is done using a sheet of mokume gane. Shapes in bright crayon colors are perfect for a child's room. As with many polymer clay projects, there are endless ways of designing this diminutive wall clock.

KNOTTY JEWELRY

Designer
Dotty McMillan

This quick and easy jewelry will get plenty of attention, not because it's naughty, but because it's very knotty. The beads are simple granny knots. It's a great way to use small leftover colors of clay.

MATERIALS

Polymer clay:

A variety of colors, about 1 oz (28 g) of each

Black, 2 oz (56 g)

Needle tool

Sharp blade

Pasta machine (optional)

Clay-compatible glaze

Elastic or bead wire

Jewelry clasps (optional)

Spacer beads of your choice

1. Condition the colors using the pasta machine or by hand. To make a many-colored bead, roll out each color except black, making snakes about ⅛" (3 mm) in diameter. Roll out the black clay in a snake that is about ⅜" (1 cm) in diameter. Surround the black snake with as many colored snakes as will fit around it (Photo 1). Leave a space between the colors where the black shows through. Roll the assembled piece down to a cane about ¼" to ¹⁄₁₆" (6 to 1.5 mm) in diameter. Cut the cane into 5" (12.5 cm) long pieces.

2. If the clay is warm and soft, refrigerate it for a few minutes to firm it up. Otherwise it tends to stick before you are able to snug the knots. Take one of the 5" lengths and tie a simple knot in the center of it. Tie again, making a double knot (Photo 2).

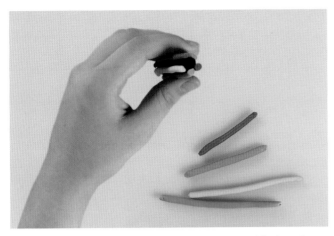

1. Putting the colors together around the center black snake.

2. Making a knot from the twisted cane length, starting at the top of the photo. The lowest one is the finished knot.

3. Stretch out the leftover knot ends slightly and trim them if necessary to about ¼" (6 mm) in length. Tuck each end in wherever it looks good, to finish your knotted bead. Keep making beads the same way. Vary the sizes and colors if you like. Make some that are all one color of clay if you wish.

4. Decide what size you wish the bracelet to be. I used 7 beads; you may need more. Lay out the beads and add spacer beads until you get the line of them to the right length. Remember to leave room for a clasp if you are using bead wire. If you are using elastic, you can make the length shorter. Make beads for a necklace the same way to go with your bracelet, about 15 beads.

5. Use the needle tool to make a hole through the knotted beads. Pick any spot you like to place the hole. Bake the beads on a piece of card stock and let cool. Glaze them if you want shiny beads and let dry. Lay out and assemble the bracelet. Use spacer beads in between if you wish.

I've made these knotted beads in all black, antiqued with cadmium red acrylic paint; in pearl, silver, and black colors; and in rainbow colors. All these colors worked well. Go ahead. Get knotty!

DECORATIVE MASK

Designer
Dotty McMillan

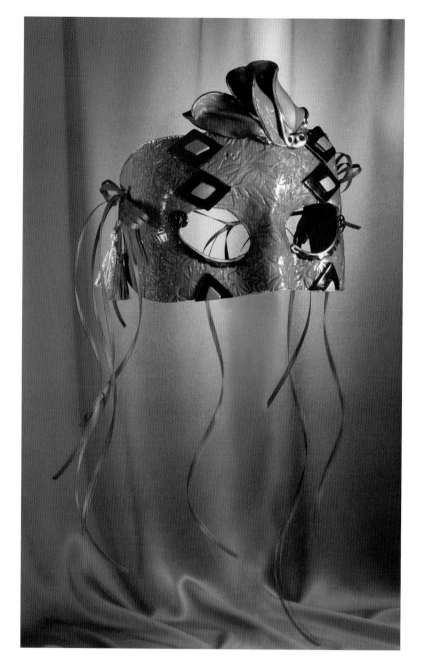

The use of masks dates back to earliest history; humans have always been aware of the power of the mask. Masks have two main purposes: to conceal the identity of the wearer, usually by representing another person or creature, and to protect the wearer. The variety of mask styles is enormous. Many are quite simple to make. They can stimulate creativity for many people.

The half-mask offered here echoes Mardi gras, parties, festivals, and masked balls. Half-masks are lighter and easier to wear than full masks. They are also easy to make once you have a face mold.

MATERIALS

Polymer clay:

       Waste clay, at least 1 pound (454 g)

       Red, 3 oz (84 g)

       Metallic gold, 3 oz (84 g)

       Black, 1 oz (28 g)

Face mold (or plaster gauze and face cream if you are making one from a person's face)

Texture sheet or rubber stamp

Aluminum foil

Ribbons and cord for decorating and wearing the mask

Polyester batting

Diamond-shaped petit four cutters in several sizes

Oval cutter for eyes (optional)

Wet/dry sandpaper, 320 and 400 grits

Clear liquid acrylic glaze

Krylon gold acrylic pen (optional)

Pattern scissors (optional)

Craft knife

Paper and pencil

Pasta machine

1. Get or make a mold.

a. You will need some type of a full face mold, which can be used for both half- and full-sized masks. There are some wonderful glass heads that can often be found at import stores. The face area of one of these can be used to make a waste clay polymer clay mold. Just stretch a large sheet of waste clay rolled out on the #1 setting (⅛" or 3.2 mm) of the pasta machine over the glass face. Carefully press the clay into the features

of the face. Smooth and tuck as necessary until you are happy with the shape of the face. Lay the clay-covered glass head onto a bed of polyester batting and bake. Be sure the piece is cool before removing it from the glass, to avoid ripping the clay. Rips can be mended with cyanoacrylate glue, however.

b. Porcelain or pottery wall masks will work well as molds also. Cover these with aluminum foil and then follow the directions above to make your mold.

c. If none of these are available in your area, you could use a real person's face and plaster gauze. This takes a bit more time but is worth the effort. Find someone who is willing to be your model. Then cover the model's face with an oil-based face cream and have the person cover his or her hair with a shower cap. Cut the gauze into strips, dip into water, and lay strips so that they cover the entire face, except for the nostrils and eye area. Continue placing the strips until you have built up at least 3 layers. Let the gauze dry until it is sturdy enough to be removed. Set aside to dry with a bundle of polyester batting inside to support the arch of the face. This will give you a full face mask that can be used to create either a full mask or a half-mask.

d. Making the clay mold. When the gauze is completely dry, cover it with a sheet of aluminum foil and then with a sheet of waste clay that has been rolled out on the #1 (⅛") setting of the pasta machine. Do not press too hard, as extra pressure may cause the plaster mask to crack. Keep one hand underneath to support the areas where you are pressing in the clay, such as around the nose, mouth, and eyes. Very carefully lift the foil and clay off the plaster mask, fill the inside with batting, and set the piece face up in the oven. Make sure it is sitting evenly so that the face does not dip or bend where it shouldn't. Bake for 1 hour at the recommended temperature. When cool, cover the entire mold with aluminum foil, tucking it inside the bottom to keep it in place (Photo 1). You now have a clay mold that you can use over and over.

1. Mold for making masks being covered in aluminum foil.

2. Shaping the textured clay mask over the mold.

2. Prepare the clay for your half-mask. Roll out a sheet of the red clay on the #1 setting. Roll out a sheet of the metallic clay on the #1 setting. Trim these sheets to about 5" × 8" long (12.7 × 17.8 cm). Stack them together with the red clay on top. Run them through the pasta machine, cut in half, and stack. Do this 3 times.

3. Use a texture sheet or rubber stamp to texture the surface of the clay sheet. If you are using a texture sheet, leave 1" of untextured clay at each end. This is necessary as the texture sheets are about 2" (5 cm) too short for the length of the clay sheet needed.

4. After texturing, slice off the raised surfaces over the entire sheet (see instructions for shaving in dragon skin mokume gane section, pages 39 to 40).

5. Trim the sheet to 4½" (11.3 cm) high by 11" (28 cm) wide. Cut a curve at each end of the mask as shown in the pattern, and cut small holes for cord or ribbons. Use an oval cutter to cut the eyeholes, or cut with a craft knife. Save the eye pieces you removed and set aside.

6. Lay the textured, mask-shaped clay sheet across the middle of the foil-covered face mold with the bottom edge just a little below the end of the nose. Begin pressing the clay into the nose, mouth, and eye areas (Photo 2). Do this slowly and gently so as not to tear the clay. Coax the clay to fit smoothly against the curved sides of the face. Trim the side ends so that they will not lie on the baking surface.

7. Cut out various shapes of black and gold clay and apply to the face (see Photo 3). The black and gold diamonds shown here are made with diamond-shaped petit four cutters. Use pattern scissors or a craft knife to cut out the lower lid eyelashes from a #3 (3⁄32" or 2.4 mm) sheet of black clay. Use the clay cut from the eyeholes to make the twisted "feathers" for the top of the mask. Make a third feather by cutting another piece the same size and shape as the eyehole pieces. To make the twists, lay the ovals onto a sheet of #1 black clay. Cut around each oval. Run each oval lengthwise through the pasta machine on the #1 setting, which will lengthen them. Twist each lengthened oval a turn or two and then fasten it down snugly to the top of the mask.

3. Starting to decorate.

8. Place the mask on its mold in the oven and bake for 1 hour at the recommended temperature. When the mask is cool, remove it from the mold. You can use your mask as is by attaching a cord or ribbons so it can be worn. Or go over it with 320 and 400 grit wet/dry sandpaper, including the edges. Coat the entire front surface with clear liquid acrylic glaze. (Some floor finishes work well for this.) Do not use a spray, as the propellant will react badly with the clay. Two coats or more are best. This will give your mask a glass-like finish.

9. If you like, use a gold Krylon pen to gild the edges of the mask and eyeholes. (This brand of pen is compatible with the clay.) When the mask is completely dry, add ribbons and cord, even some dangly beads, and have fun wearing your mask. Or use it as a wall decoration.

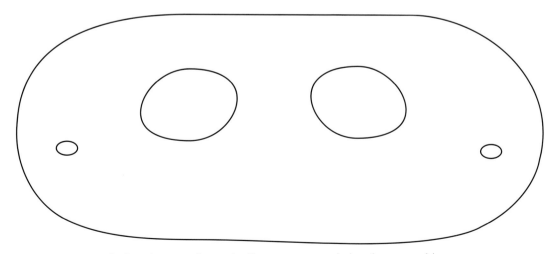

Reduced pattern for mask. Copy at size needed to fit your mold.

LIGHT-BULB VESSEL

Designer
Dotty McMillan

*H*ow many burned-out light bulbs have you tossed away without realizing that they are perfect armatures for making polymer clay vessels? The glass bulb is removed after the piece is baked. This is an easy and delightful way to make a small vessel, using just about any surface technique or colors that you like.

MATERIALS

Polymer clay:

> Black, 4 oz (112 g)

> Blue, 3 oz (84 g)

> Purple, 1 oz

> Plain pearl, tiny bit

> Liquid clay

Plastic texture sheet with small, overall pattern, or other texturing tool

Spray bottle and water

Several small molds, such as a small flower or a fancy button

Sharp blade or craft knife

Needle tool

Small oval cutter and circle cutter, 1½" (3.8 cm), optional

Pasta machine or acrylic roller

Wet/dry sandpaper, 320 and 400 grits

Regular 32-grit sandpaper, small piece

Clay-compatible glaze

Gold mica powder

Paper bags

Hammer

Old light bulb, 75-watt size

Safety goggles

Buffing equipment

1. Condition the various colors of clay. Roll out a sheet of black on the #3 setting (³⁄₃₂" or 2.4 mm) of the pasta machine or use a roller.

2. Hold the light bulb with the metal screw end up. Cover the glass portions of the bulb with the black clay (Photo 1). Do not cover any part of the metal screw. Cut, shape, and smooth the clay to fit the curves of the bulb. Trim off any excess. Use a piece of very rough sandpaper to texture all the black clay on the bulb. Roll a ball of black clay 1¼" (3.1 cm) in diameter, and flatten it so that it is about ¾" (2 cm) thick and about 1½" (3.8 cm) in diameter. Attach this flat pad on the round end of the bulb, over the area that carries the writing. This will be the base of your vessel.

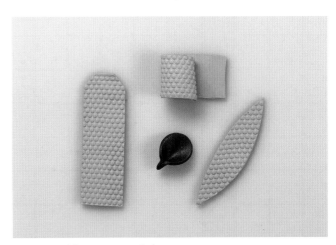

2. Basic add-on pieces of clay.

1. The light bulb is covered in black clay, shown before excess was trimmed off.

3. A curled leaf piece is attached to the black clay.

3. Roll out the blue clay on the #1 (⅛" or 3.2 mm) setting of the pasta machine. Texture the entire surface. If you use a plastic texture sheet, spray its surface with water, lay the clay against it, and run it through the pasta machine on the #1 setting or roll over the clay and texture sheet together with an acrylic roller.

4. To make the curled leaves, cut out 4 strips of the textured blue clay, each 1½" (3.8 cm) × 4" (10 cm). Trim the corners off one short end of each at an angle (Photo 2, left). Place the straight edge of a strip against the side of the clay-covered light bulb near the bottom. Curl the piece so that the angle-cut end is inside. Press this piece against the black clay (Photo 3). Place the other two strips around the bulb at equal distances from each other.

5. With the remaining blue clay, make a new textured sheet. Cut out 4 narrow ovals that are 4" long. Place these over the black clay of the vase, in between the curled leaves. (You can see the finished vase in Photo 5.)

6. To make flowers, cut four 1¼" × 1" (3.1 × 2.5 cm) ovals from a sheet of black clay, using oval cutters or by hand. Pinch the bottom edges of each oval together. These are your flowers. You can see them in the opener photo. Roll out 4 narrow snakes of black clay that are 1" (2.5 cm) long and pointed at one end. These are the flower stamens. Place a stamen inside each flower. Gild the edges of the flower and the stamen with gold mica powder. Place one flower at the top edge of each curled leaf (see opener photo). Add small balls of purple clay and pearl clay between each leaf and its flower.

7. Roll out 4 small balls of black clay, sized to fit inside a curled blue leaf. Gently insert one inside each curl.

8. For decorations around the base, press purple clay into a small flower mold (or any other small decorative mold), and gild the raised edge of each flower with gold mica powder. Add the molded pieces, equally spaced around the bottom edge, over the blue clay pieces on the vase (Photo 4). Bake the piece and let cool.

5. Hit downwards on the metal part to break the bulb.

4. View of finished vase from the bottom.

9. To remove the glass bulb from inside the vessel, place the vase inside two layers of paper bag with only the metal screw portion outside. Wear safety goggles. Hold the bag and vessel straight up in one hand, with the bottom against a hard surface such as concrete. With the hammer in your other hand, bang down hard on the top of the metal screw portion of the bulb (Photo 5). Turn the bag and vessel so that the side of the metal shows, and give the metal another bang. Be careful at this point, as there will be glass shards inside the paper bag. Carefully remove the metal screw portion. Lift out the vessel and dump any loose glass into the bag. Sometimes most of the glass will break away from the clay. Other times it may be stubborn and stick somewhat. Use a small knife to carefully pry off the remaining glass. Rinse out the inside of the vessel to make certain it is free of shards.

10. With blue clay, make a small snake, notch it with your needle tool, bend into a circle, and add to the top edge of the vessel. It helps if you add a small amount of liquid clay between the baked and the unbaked clay. Bake the piece again.

11. For the lid, cut a 1½" (3.8 cm) circle from blue clay that has been put through the pasta machine on the #1 setting. Roll a small ball of black clay and flatten it somewhat. See if the black clay will fit into the opening of the vessel. It will be the stop for the lid. Keep working with it until you get a piece that fits well. Add this flattened piece to the bottom of the blue clay circle. Use black clay to roll out a narrow

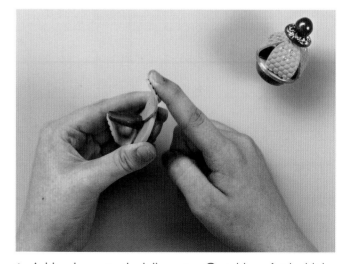

6. Adding leaves to the lid's center. On table, a finished lid.

ARTFUL WAYS WITH POLYMER CLAY

cone-shaped piece about ¾" (1.9 cm) tall. Place this cone in the center of the blue circle as the centerpiece of the lid. From a small sheet of textured blue clay, cut out four 1½" × 1¼" (3.8 x 3.2 cm) ovals. Curl them to fit against the center piece of the lid as shown (Photo 6).

12. Mold a small round decorative piece of black clay, flatten it, and place on top of the centerpiece and blue curls. Add a small ball of purple clay on the top (Photo 6). Bake and let cool.

13. Coat the flowers and stamens, the molded pieces, and the small ball on the top with a clay-compatible glaze. Sand and buff the bottom of the vessel.

Your vessel is finished and ready to stand on a shelf or desk. You can vary the width and length of the curled leaves, flowers, etc. for a different look. Narrower decorative pieces make the vessel look daintier, as seen in the green vessel in Photo 7. The light bulb as armature concept is very versatile. You could also make a vessel entirely of canes, as shown on the right in Photo 7.

7. Three light-bulb vessels. The one at right is made of cane slices.

Gallery of Artists' Work

Swirl Pin
by Tracy van Buskirk.

Gilded Egg Box and Pendant
by Patricia Kimle.

Earth Textures Ikebana Vase
by Mona Kissel.

Tribal Style Mask
by Carol Zilliacus.

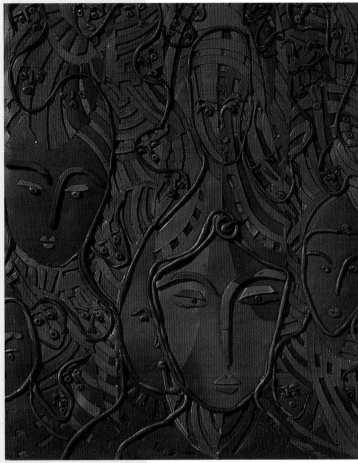

Faces
by Carol Zilliacus.

Switchplate covers
by Tracy Van Buskirk.

Treasure Chest
by Denita Johnson.
Photo by Shannon Ritchardson.

Polymer Clay Stick Figure
by Vicki Rhine.

Multi-Caned Teapot
by Denita Johnson.
Photo by Shannon Ritchardson.

Grandma's Table
polymer clay painting
by Cassie Doyon.

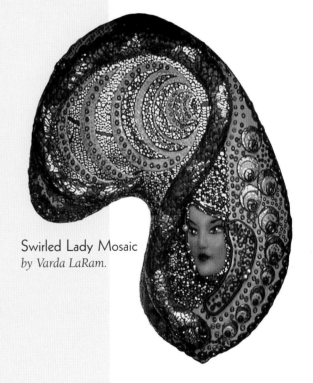

Swirled Lady Mosaic
by Varda LaRam.

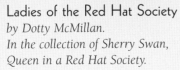

Ladies of the Red Hat Society
by Dotty McMillan.
In the collection of Sherry Swan,
Queen in a Red Hat Society.

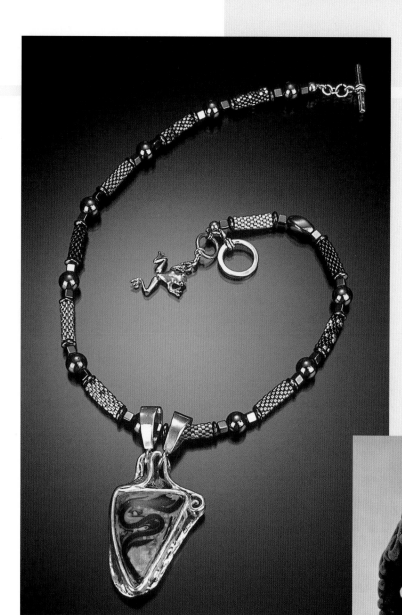

Zygote
by Arlene Schiek.

Khat-Fishing
by Lashonne Abel.
Precious metal clay and
polymer clay. Photo by
Robes & Diamante.

Filigree Egg
by Marcella Brooks. Photo by
Gordon McCarty.

Shirt and scarf buckles
by Dotty McMillan.

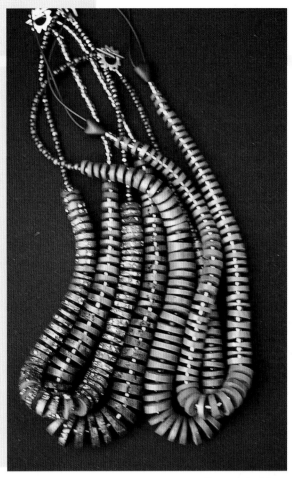

Slices Necklace
by Mona Kissel.

Smooch Bowl
by Denita Johnson.
Photo by Shannon
Ritchardson.

Autumn Fairy
by Kathy Davis.

Sunday's Ride
by Kathy Davis.

Blue Dragon
by Jane Zhao.

Box
by Jane Zhao.

White Dragon
by Jane Zhao.

Flowered Vase with
Red Roses
by Linda Hess.

Hand and Face Pin *by Pam Rouleau.*

Kitties with Quilts
by Deborah Anderson.

GALLERY OF ARTISTS' WORK

Dry-Fall Kaleidoscopes
by Dotty McMillan.

Rainsticks
by Dotty McMillan.

Midnight Lace Wheel Kaleidoscope
by Dotty McMillan.

Poinsettia cane on dragon-skin box
by Trina Williams.

Evening bag
made over
large matchbox
*by Dotty
McMillan.*

Sepia-toned brooch
by Dotty McMillan.

Index